PONTIFICAL SWISS GUARD

PRESENTS

THE

VATICAN COOKBOOK

FIRST EDITION

Contributing Authors
David Geisser, Erwin Niederberger & Thomas Kelly
Photographs
All photographs by Katarzyna Artymiak, except as noted on Page 201 (Photography).
Translations
Archangel Press
Supervising Editor
Thomas Kelly
Editorial Editor
Michael Dunigan
Copy Editors
Valerie Maczak, Eva Beyeler
IT & Graphic Director
Michael Criscione
Graphic Design
Nina Ruosch, Nicholas Bresler
Layout
Margreth Zuber, Anne Sheehan
Cover Design
Carolyn McKinney, Archangel Productions
Image Processing
Adrian Aellig
Correctors
Uschi Baumgartner, Sheila Perry
Recipe & Culinary Advisor
Gerard Grim, Jr.
Photographic Advisor
Julianna Walborn

Pontifical Swiss Guard presents The Vatican Cookbook is a modified edition of the original Swiss publication, *Pontifical Swiss Guard – Buon Appetito*, published in Switzerland (2014) by Werd & Weber Verlag AG.

PONTIFICAL SWISS GUARD – BUON APPETITO
© 2014 Werd & Weber Verlag AG, CH-3645 Thun/Gwatt (www.weberverlag.ch)
All rights reserved, including all rights to use of excerpts for any purpose and to all electronic renditions.

German Edition: ISBN 978-3-03818-016-6
French Edition: ISBN 978-3-03818-066-1
Italian Editon: ISBN 978-3-03818-067-8

Published by: Guardia Svizzera Pontifica
Città del Vaticano 00120
gsp@gsp.va

SOPHIA
INSTITUTE PRESS

www.SophiaInstitute.com

North American Edition: ISBN 978-1-622823-321
Published by: Sophia Institute Press
Box 5284, Manchester, NH 03108
1-800-888-9344

Sophia Institute Press® is a registered trademark of Sophia Institute.

FIRST EDITION
1 3 5 7 9 10 8 6 4 2

PONTIFICAL SWISS GUARD

PRESENTS

THE

VATICAN

COOKBOOK

David Geisser
Erwin Niederberger
Thomas Kelly

*500 Years of Classic Recipes, Papal Tributes and
Exclusive Images of Life and Art at the Vatican*

SOPHIA INSTITUTE PRESS
Manchester, New Hampshire

CONTENTS

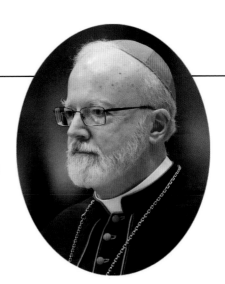

My Dear Friends,

Throughout the Scriptures, there are many accounts of the importance and benefits of extending hospitality. In the Old Testament and the New Testament, men and women from the Jewish and Christian traditions are noted for welcoming visitors, those known and those only just met, with the invitation to share their homes and their tables as a sign of gratitude for the blessings they have received in life.

By way of this wonderful book the Pontifical Swiss Guard of the Holy See has provided a means to plan time together with family, friends and new acquaintances. Gathering around a table for a well prepared meal – and this book makes it possible for any of us to present that setting, whatever our level of culinary skill – is a means of sharing fellowship and getting to know one another better.

Any home or residence would be graced by a copy of "Pontifical Swiss Guard Presents the Vatican Cookbook," which also would be a very thoughtful and well received gift for family or friends. It is my hope that this book will help people come together to share the goodness of the Lord.

Asking God's blessings on you and all whom you hold dear, I am,

Sincerely yours,

Cardinal Seàn O'Malley, OFM, Cap.

Archbishop of Boston

FOREWORD

For more than 500 years, young men of Switzerland have been honored to serve as guardians of the Pope at the Vatican in Rome and Defenders of the Faith. The Pontifical Swiss Guard stands proud today as the last of a long and storied tradition of elite Swiss soldiers, sworn to duty in this most special service far from their families and their homes in Switzerland.

Through the centuries, the Pontifical Swiss Guard has been responsible for the safety of the Supreme Pontiff of the Catholic Church and of the security of His residence in Vatican City.

We pay tribute to the sons of the homeland, volunteers all, the noble ones stepping forward from every canton of Switzerland, following in the footsteps of their fathers and ancestors on the path to Rome. The standards are very high. Discipline, motivation and readiness must be exemplary. If they meet all qualifications, they may be granted the honor of wearing the colors of the Guard for a tour of duty in service to the Holy Father.

This Book offers the reader a special inside look behind the walls of Vatican City through the eyes of the Swiss Guardsmen. Stroll through the Vatican Gardens. Walk the hallowed halls of St. Peter's. Behold the fine art of the ages at the Vatican Museums. Meet the officers of the Guard and the leaders of the Holy See. Join us at holiday celebrations. Learn of the Swiss Guard legends and traditions handed down over generations, since the days of Michelangelo.

Security and defense duties are paramount for the Guard, but in this Book, there is something more, something special. It is about a simple but essential part of life, not just for the Guard, but for everyone. It is the food. For the Guard, it is also appropriate in a special cookbook such as this to support organizations that campaign for an end to hunger in the world and for fair distribution of food. As Pope Francis tells us, food is a basic human right.

The Swiss Guard is pleased and proud to present this assortment of recipes for meals of all occasions. With this Book, we want to offer a gift: the joy of the culinary arts, the perpetual preparation and presentation of food for our meals, and to acknowledge the responsibility we all have to end world hunger.

And we welcome the reader with the simple Swiss Guard motto that inspires us always in the way we serve and the way we live — *Acriter et Fideliter — Most Courageous and Most Faithful!*

— Colonel Christoph Graf
Commander

INTRODUCTION

A cookbook with the Pontifical Swiss Guard?

What has the one to do with the other? That was my first reaction when I heard the surprising proposal for a Swiss Guard Vatican Cookbook. It wasn't long before I realized that this had the makings of a very special project.

A Swiss Guard Book had been in the works for years, beginning with the concept for a modest publication to promulgate the honor and benefits of Guard service in the Swiss homeland. Past, present and future, all Guardsmen hail from Switzerland and the officers of the Guard are obliged to encourage young Swiss recruits.

The scope of our project changed dramatically in 2012 when David Geisser joined the Guard. With the prodigy chef, we have a young man with remarkable culinary skills and a talent for writing. Twice already, he has lived through that most difficult process, the rendering of a cookbook, succeeding on both occasions. It was David who led the way from Book to Cookbook.

At the same time, we enlisted the services of Katarzyna Artymiak, the stellar Vatican photographer. From the grandest scale to the finest detail, her marvelous photographs bring the Book to life.

There were more welcome contributions from many in the Guard as work progressed: personal stories, holiday memories, first hand historical accounts and more enhancements in words and pictures.

Now, our little brochure has been transformed into a wonderful cookbook and so much more. We make the acquaintance of some prominent personalities of the Holy See, learn the history and legends of the Swiss Guard, enjoy the magnificent art and tour the special places of Vatican City.

The highlight has to be our tributes to the three Holy Fathers we have served in the modern era, and the revelation of delicious Vatican secrets — favorite dishes of Pope Francis, Pope Benedict XVI and Holy Pope John Paul II.

Our Book concludes with table prayers and a simple plea: Join the Swiss Guard in support of *One Human Family, Food for All*, the campaign to end hunger in the world that Pope Francis has endorsed in the strongest terms. The blessing of good food is meant to be shared. Learn more about *Food for All* in the final pages of this Book.

And we wish you, dear readers, friends, and friends of the Guard, much joy in reading the stories and discovering the wonders of the Vatican, and especially in the making and partaking of the recipes.

Buon Appetito from the Swiss Guard!

— Sergeant Erwin Niederberger

THE SWEARING-IN

It is in solemn memory of the Sacco di Roma, the plundering of Rome by the renegade army of the German Emperor Charles V and the legendary Stand of the Guard in defense of the Holy Father, that the annual swearing-in ceremony takes place on the Sixth of May. With the taking of the oath, right hand raised high in the three-fingered salute that symbolizes the Holy Trinity of the Church, the young men become Swiss Guards, and swear to faithfully serve and honor the Pope and His legitimate successors, and to give of all their strength and even their lives to this pledge.

For some, it is a brief affiliation with the corps, a single 25-month tour of duty before returning to their private lives. For others, service in the Guard becomes a career choice, dedication of 25 years or more to the noble cause. Regardless, active service may come to an end, but in the heart, every man remains always a Guardsman.

At the Vatican, the Sixth of May is one of the most important dates on the calendar every year. There are weeks of preparation for the special events of the day. In addition to the entire complement of the Guard and the families and friends of the newly sworn, there are many important dignitaries from the Church, political and secular officials and others present.

The full oath is read aloud by the Swiss Guard Chaplain:

> "I swear I will faithfully, loyally, and honorably serve the Supreme Pontiff Francis and His legitimate Successors, and also dedicate myself to Them with all my strength, sacrificing if necessary also my life to defend Them. I assume this same commitment with regard to the Sacred College of Cardinals whenever the See is vacant.
>
> "Furthermore I promise respect, fidelity and obedience to the Commanding Captain and my other Superiors.
>
> "This I swear! May God and our Holy Patrons assist me."

The oath is repeated in a shortened form by each of the new recruits.

> "I swear I will observe faithfully, loyally, and honorably all that has been read out to me! May God and our Holy Patrons assist me."

The day of the swearing-in is surely a high point in the life of every member of the Guard. Anyone who has worn the Gran Gala Uniform and marched under the flag of the Pontifical Swiss Guard carries the oath for the rest of his life. It is an oath which avows commitment to bravery and fidelity above all, an oath with an obligation of complete devotion and loyalty. In the tradition that has prevailed for five centuries, from the moment the words are spoken, each and all are Swiss Guards now and forever.

Today the Pontifical Swiss Guard has a complement of 110 men.

GIRANDOLE FOR THE SIXTH OF MAY

Ingredients

4	Tomatoes, peeled, diced ½ inch
8	Spears white asparagus
8	Spears green asparagus
4	Whole scallions (green stalk and bulbs)
2 Tbs.	Olive oil
2 Tbs.	Noilly Prat (dry vermouth)
½ cup	Heavy cream
0.10 oz.	Saffron threads
1 lb.	Girandole (long corkscrew pasta)
	Sea salt
	Fresh ground black pepper

Serves 4

Preparation

Bring a pot with 3 quarts of salted water to a low boil. Cross cut the bottom of each tomato, and blanch briefly in the hot water (about 1 to 2 minutes). Transfer the tomatoes to ice water for 1 minute to stop the cooking process. Do not discard the water; it will be used to cook the pasta. Peel the tomato skins, cut into quarters, remove the seeds and dice into ½-inch pieces.

Peel the very thin outer layer of the white and green asparagus, and trim about 1 inch from the bottoms.

Cook the pasta in the salted water to al dente. In the meantime, slice the scallions into thin rings. Heat the olive oil over medium heat, and sauté the scallions for about 2 minutes. Pour in the dry vermouth (Noilly Prat), and then add the heavy cream and saffron threads. Bring the liquid to a boil, and reduce the heat to low. Season to taste with the sea salt and pepper.

Drain the cooked pasta, and add it to the cream. Toss gently to cover the pasta with the sauce. Garnish with diced tomato.

The Sixth of May is the most important date on the Swiss Guard calendar. We remember the valiant ones who have fallen in defense of Vatican freedom as we welcome the new Guardsmen to our ranks. It is both a solemn and joyful day, attended by the entire corps of the Guard, family and friends, many Vatican dignitaries and distinguished guests from Rome and beyond. The culmination is always the dinner and reception, often held in the Vatican Museums. Can you imagine the good fortune to be seated at the beautifully appointed tables surrounded by magnificent works of Michelangelo, Leonardo da Vinci, Raphael and the finest art treasures of 20 centuries? It is an unforgettable experience.

FILET OF BEEF TAGLIATA

Ingredients

Filet of Beef:

1	Sprig of fresh thyme
1	Garlic clove
2 Tbs.	Olive oil
2 ½ lbs.	Beef tenderloin
	Sea salt

Chantarelles:

1	Large tomato, peeled, diced ½ inch
½ lb.	Chanterelle mushrooms
1	Shallot, minced
2 Tbs.	Olive oil
1 Tbs.	Fresh thyme leaves, finely chopped
	Fresh ground black pepper

Salad:

2 oz.	Arugula
	Juice of half a lime
1 Tbs.	Good balsamic vinegar
2 Tbs.	Good virgin olive oil
3 oz.	Shaved Parmesan

Serves 4

Preparation

Preheat the oven to 425°. Bring a pot with 2 quarts of salted water to a low boil. Cross cut the bottom of each tomato, and blanch briefly in the hot water (about 1 to 2 minutes). Transfer the tomatoes to ice water for 1 minute to stop the cooking process. Peel the tomato skins, cut into quarters, remove the seeds and dice into ½-inch pieces.

Season the beef with salt and pepper. Heat about 2 Tbs. of olive oil in a large oven-safe pan over medium heat. Sauté the sprig of thyme and whole garlic clove for about 1 minute, stirring often. Add the tenderloin to the pan, and brown on all sides, about 1 to 2 minutes per side. Place the beef in the oven, and cook for about 40-45 minutes to a meat thermometer temperature of 130°.

In the meantime, wash and dry the arugula. Clean and trim the ends of the mushrooms with a small kitchen knife. Mince the shallot. Strip the leaves from the second thyme sprig, and finely chop. Heat about 2 Tbs. of olive oil over high heat. Add the mushrooms to the pan and sauté. Stir vigorously. After about 1 minute, add the shallots, diced tomato and thyme leaves to the mushrooms. Season with salt and pepper to taste.

For the salad, to make the dressing whisk the premium olive oil, balsamic vinegar and lime juice together in a bowl. Season with salt and pepper. Pour over the arugula, and toss gently. Move the dressed arugula to a plate with a paper towel on it to dry the leaves slightly.

Remove the tenderloin from the oven and let it rest at least 5 minutes. Slice the rested beef. Arrange a bed of the dressed arugula on the serving plates. Place two slices of tenderloin on each plate. Spoon the sautéed mushrooms over the beef, sprinkle the shaved Parmesan on top, and serve immediately.

The Swiss Chef recommends: potatoes au gratin.

BAVARESE YOGURT & STRAWBERRY COULIS

Ingredients

Bavarese:

0.25 oz.	Unflavored leaf gelatin
3 ½ oz.	Heavy cream
1	Vanilla bean
5 oz.	Milk
2	Egg yolks
3 ½ Tbs.	Raw cane sugar
4 oz.	Plain yogurt

Strawberry Coulis:

¾ cup	Hulled strawberries
3 ½ Tbs.	Raw cane sugar
2 Tbs.	Cognac (Grand Marnier)

Serves 4

Preparation

Place the leaf gelatin into a small bowl with cold water and let it soak. Whisk the cream in another bowl until frothy and firm, either by hand or using a mixer.

Cut the vanilla bean in half lengthwise and scrape out the seeds. Warm the milk in a saucepan over medium heat to a near boil, and then add the vanilla bean slices.

Remove the gelatin from the water. Dissolve it into the warm milk and whisk to a rich texture. Make sure the milk is not too hot.

In a bowl, beat the egg yolks with the sugar until frothy and they shine a bright yellow. Slowly pour the warm milk through a fine mesh filter into the yolk-sugar mix, stirring constantly. Set the mixture aside to cool to room temperature. Then add the yogurt.

As soon as the mix begins to set, fold in the whipped cream. Pour the mix into 4 parfait glasses and refrigerate until firm.

Just before serving, purée the strawberries, sugar and cognac, and pour over the Bavarese in the individual glasses, creating a thick surface. Serve with whole strawberries or chocolates.

THE SWISS GUARD IN SERVICE TO THE POPES

The papal alliance with the Swiss Guard began in 1505 when Pope Julius II sent an urgent request to the Swiss Diet for a company of Swiss Guards to protect the Holy Father and the home of the Church in Rome. The decision to enlist Swiss soldiers did not come by chance. It was an age of turbulence, with wars and conflicts, large and small, raging across Europe. The new Pope was determined to protect the interests and integrity of the Church and the safety of the Pontiff himself. By virtue of their fidelity and ferocity in battle, the Swiss were regarded as invincible, the "Most Courageous & Most Loyal" soldiers in the land. Summoned to Rome, a contingent of 150 Swiss crossed the Alps in the dead of winter, arriving on January 22, 1506. With proper ceremony, they were blessed and received by the Holy Father and assigned to quarters at the Vatican, adjacent to the Apostolic Palace. The age of the Pontifical Swiss Guard had begun.

The first great trial of the Swiss Guard came on May 6, 1527. It was the tragic time of the Sacco di Roma , the Sack of Rome. The rogue army of Emperor Charles V assaulted the city, intent on plunder and destruction. Only the Swiss Guard stood in the way. Commander Kaspar Röist led 147 Guardsmen to the last line of defense at the steps of St. Peter's Basilica, where every man gave his life to save the Holy Father. The valiant soldiers held just long enough against thousands of marauders while the last platoon of the Guard escorted Pope Clement VII through the famed secret passage, the Passetto di Borgo, and on to safety at the Castel Sant'Angelo. The legendary Stand and Sacrifice of the Swiss Guard are honored every year on the Sixth of May, the day of Swearing-In, as new recruits swear before God and man to protect the Pope with their lives.

Today, the primary responsibilities of the Guard remain virtually unchanged after 500 years. Security for the Holy Father, protection of His person and vigilance over His residence are the first and foremost orders of the day.

There are other important duties: guarding the entrances to Vatican City, enforcement of the laws, and security provisions for the Holy Father on his international travels.

In case of a Vacant See, a vacancy in the Papal Chair, the allegiance of the Swiss Guard is subordinated to the Sacred College of Cardinals. The Guard takes full responsibility for their security pending the election of the new Pope.

Every member of the Guard is a citizen of the Vatican City state, thus governed by Vatican law, including the military rules of the Guard and the orders of the Swiss Guard's Commander. The Guardsman is honor bound to loyalty, respect and vigilance, and always ready to serve. It is the duty of the Guardsman to recognize his solemn obligations in all religious, moral and military regards, with a daily commitment to perfection.

POPE FRANCIS

Jorge Mario Bergoglio
266th Successor to Saint Peter
Pontifical Father from March 13, 2013

Born in Argentina, first of five children of an Italian immigrant family, Jorge Mario Bergoglio was a talented child and a gifted student who earned a degree in chemical engineering and began work in that field at an early age. But he soon found his calling to the priesthood. After years of scholastic instruction and theological studies, Bergoglio was ordained to the Jesuit Order in 1969. He continued his advanced education in Spain, Germany and Ireland, always returning to pastoral work in Argentina. Bergoglio rose rapidly to positions of honor and authority: Confessor and Provincial of the Jesuit Order in Cordoba, Bishop and Archbishop of the Diocese of Buenos Aires and Jesuit Vicar General. In 2001, he was elevated to Cardinal.

After the resignation of Pope Benedict XVI, it was astonishing news when Cardinal Bergoglio was selected as the 266th Successor to Saint Peter on March 13, 2013, the first non-European pope in more than 1,200 years, the first ever from the Americas, and the first to take the name Francis.

Pope Francis has continued to astonish the world since his first greeting from the Benediction loge of St. Peter's: buona sera, a casual "good evening to you all." He lives in the *Domus Sanctae Marthae*, modest guesthouse of the Apostolic Palace, grand home of his predecessors. He favors unadorned white vestments and has worn the same simple cross for years. The humility, good will and soft-spoken wisdom of Pope Francis set an example for us all.

The lifestyle of Pope Francis aligns with his lifelong commitment to the poor, the underprivileged and the sick at heart. He has made it his mission to act as the champion of all those on the margins of society and is their most powerful voice as well, speaking out time and again against the scandals of poverty and hunger in an affluent world. At the same time, he has taken a leading role on the world stage as an arbiter and peacemaker, helping to resolve disputes between great nations and build bridges among people of all cultures and faiths.

The effortless style of charismatic Pope Francis has fascinated the public and the media from the earliest days of his papacy, with his every word and deed making for headline news around the globe. And yet he remains the kind and approachable pastor with a wise word and a gentle smile for all.

We present Pope Francis with selections from both Argentine and Italian menus as a tribute to his homeland and his heritage. We know that Cardinal Bergoglio was no stranger to the kitchen, often preparing and serving meals for himself and others. We hope our offerings will be as pleasing to the Holy Father as his own cooking.

ARGENTINE EMPANADAS ON PEPPER SALAD

Ingredients

Hot Pepper Salad:

1	Hot red pepper, thin sliced
1	Hot yellow pepper, thin sliced
½	Shallot, thin sliced
10	Cherry tomatoes, halved
1 Tbs	Capers, minced
1 Tbs	Flat-leaf parsley, chopped fine
2 Tbs	Olive oil
1 Tbs	White balsamic vinegar
	Sea salt
	Fresh ground black pepper

Empanadas:

½ lb.	Ground beef sirloin
¼ cup	Pine nuts
¼ cup	Black olives
¼ cup	Raisins
2	Eggs, beaten
1	Sheet of puff pastry dough, unrolled
1	Egg yolk, beaten
	Sea salt
	Fresh ground black pepper

Serves 2 to 4

Preparation

Wash the peppers, remove the seeds and the white core, and cut into thin slices. Cut the shallot into thin slices. Cut the cherry tomatoes in half, and mince the capers.

For the dressing, whisk the chopped parsley, olive oil, and white balsamic vinegar together. Season with salt and pepper to taste. Then, add the peppers, shallots, tomatoes and capers to the dressing.

Pre-heat the oven to 350°. For the empanadas, brown the ground beef and drain. Put the cooked ground beef into a bowl and set it aside. In a clean pan, toast the pine nuts on low heat with no oil for about 2 to 3 minutes, stirring often and watching carefully so they do not burn. Chop the black olives. Add the toasted pine nuts, the olives, the raisins and the 2 whole eggs to the bowl with the cooked beef. Mix to combine all ingredients, and season to taste.

With a round cookie cutter (about 3-inch diameter), cut out 12 shapes from the puff pastry. Place about a tablespoon of the beef mix on the center of each dough round, then fold over, and press the edges together neatly with a fork. Coat the empanadas with the egg yolk to help them brown, and bake for 10 minutes until golden brown.

Serve the empanadas over top of the hot pepper salad.

Pope Francis Greets Bishops of the Church at the Vatican

The ecclesiastic and diplomatic duties of the Pope are important, demanding and time-consuming. Since 2013, the Pope has traveled to more than 50 nations on five continents, spoken in person to more than 80 million people and met with the leaders of dozens of nations. The comments, opinions and pronouncements of the Holy Father on a wide range of religious, moral and social subjects make worldwide news on a regular basis. Pope Francis is one of the most influential and most admired people of our time.

Pope Francis Embraces Special Children

The Holy Pontiff's intense schedule in Rome and around the world is no obstacle to the personal commitment of Pope Francis to the underprivileged. There is always time for the poor and infirm, the troubled and disabled, with children always first and foremost. One day, Pope Francis calls on all nations to rise to the challenge of a better world and support the *One Human Family, Food for All* campaign to end hunger in the world. Soon after, the Pope takes time to wash the feet of the imprisoned, walk streets of destitution and spend precious time with children at every opportunity.

COLITA DE CUADRIL

Ingredients

1	Medium carrot, diced ½ inch
1	Onion, diced ½ inch
2	Celery stalks, diced ½ inch
2 lbs.	Beef top round roast
2 Tbs.	Canola or vegetable oil
2 Tbs.	Tomato paste
½ cup	Red wine
4 cups	Beef bouillon
¼ cup	Madeira wine
1 Tbs.	Corn starch
	Sea salt
	Fresh ground black pepper

Serves 4

Preparation

Peel the carrots and the onion. Dice the carrots, onion and celery into ½ inch pieces. Tie the beef with butcher's twine, and then season it well with salt and pepper. In a large oven-safe pot, heat the oil over medium heat, and brown the meat briefly on all sides.

Remove the meat from the pot, set it aside, and pour the excess oil from the pot. Return the pot to medium heat, and add the diced vegetables and the tomato paste. Cook for 3 to 5 minutes. Place the meat back in the pot. Pour in the red wine, and cook until it is reduced by about a quarter. Then, pour in the beef bouillon until one-third of the meat is covered by the liquid.

Cover the pot and place it in the oven at 350° for about 45 minutes for medium finish (less for rare), turning the meat occasionally to baste it in the liquid. When the meat is tender, remove it from the pot and set aside to rest, keeping it warm.

Pour the liquid from the pot through a fine mesh strainer into a saucepan over medium heat. Then, add the Madeira wine. Mix the corn starch with an equal amount of cold water, and gradually stir the corn starch liquid into the cooking sauce until it reaches the desired consistency. Season the sauce to taste with salt and pepper.

Slice the beef, and serve it with the pan sauce.

The Swiss Chef suggests: potato butternut squash purée.

DULCE DE LECHE

Ingredients

10 ½ cups Whole milk
4 cups Sugar
¼ tsp. Baking soda
½ Vanilla bean
3 Tbs. Cognac

Serves 4

Preparation

Boil the milk and the sugar in a pot until the sugar is completely dissolved. Pour the mixture through a cheesecloth filter into a deep pot. Let the mixture cook over low heat for about 1 hour, stirring often, being careful that the milk does not boil over the top of the pot, stirring occasionally with a wooden spoon.

After approximately 1 hour, the liquid will become dark, thick and syrupy. Split open the vanilla bean. Add the vanilla bean, baking soda and cognac to the milk mixture.

Reduce the heat and continue to stir until the dulce de leche reaches the desired consistency. Remove the vanilla bean. Pour the mix into dessert glasses or cups, and set aside until cooled to room temperature.

As it cools, the milk mixture will thicken to the texture of honey. Stir briefly one more time before serving with a spoon.

In the summer of 2014, there was football fever at the Vatican, people from many nations rooting for their home teams in the World Cup. Of course, the Guardsmen were no exception. From front row seats at the barracks TV, we cheered the Swiss team to victory in the opening round, setting up the showdown with Argentina, home team of Pope Francis. The Argentinians won in a close game and the Swiss had to concede defeat.

After the game, I reported for overnight duty at the entrance to the Pope's residence. Just after dawn, Pope Francis stepped from his home with a bright morning greeting, then leaned close and asked if I was sad about the match. I had to admit I wanted the Swiss to win, but I saluted Argentina for the victory. Pope Francis smiled, stepped back into his home and re-emerged with a little pastry. He smiled as he handed me the sweet gift and said he hoped it would "make the day a little better." And it does, every time I think of my personal moment with Pope Francis.

— Swiss Chef, David Geisser

ALFAJORES

Ingredients

1 ¼ cups	Cornstarch
¾ cup	All-purpose flour, plus more for dusting
1 tsp.	Baking powder
¼ tsp.	Baking soda
¼ tsp.	Sea salt
1 stick	Unsalted butter, room temperature
6 Tbs.	White sugar
2	Egg yolks
1 tsp.	Cognac
1 tsp.	Vanilla extract
2 cups	Dulce de leche
¼ cup	Powdered sugar

Serves 12 to 16 sandwiches

Preparation

Sift together the cornstarch, flour, baking powder, baking soda and salt. Beat the sugar and butter in a mixer about 2 minutes until fluffy. Add the egg yolks, and mix to incorporate. Add the cognac and vanilla. Sift the cornstarch mix into the butter mix, and work together until a crumbly dough begins to form. Shape the dough into a ball, place it in a bowl covered with plastic wrap, and let it rest for about 30 minutes.

Pre-heat the oven to 325°. Dust a flat surface with flour. Roll the rested dough until it is about ¼ inch thick. Using a 2-inch round cutter, cut out the dough circles, and place them on a baking sheet, spaced at least 1 inch apart. Bake 10 to 12 minutes until the edges begin to darken very slightly. Remove the cookies from the oven and let cool completely, about 30 minutes.

Once cooled, spread about 1 Tbs. of prepared dulce de leche on half of the cookies and use the remaining cookies to make a sandwich. Dust with powdered sugar before serving.

If I had only one wish, what would it be?

The only thing I would like is to go out one day, without being recognized, and go to a pizzeria for a pizza.

— Pope Francis (2015)

PIZZA A CABALLO

Ingredients

Pizza Dough:

½ cup	Warm water, about 110°
1 packet	Yeast (2 ¼ tsp.)
1 ¼ cups	Lukewarm water
2 Tbs.	Olive oil
4 cups	Bread flour, plus more for dusting
1 ½ tsp.	Sea salt
	Olive oil for greasing

Sauce & Toppings:

1 cup	Fresh tomato sauce
½ cup	Sliced mushrooms
½	Sliced onions
½ tsp	Oregano
1 tsp	Fresh basil
1 cup	Chopped zucchini
8 oz	Mozzarella cheese
8 slices	Faina flatbread
½ tsp.	Semolina flour

Serves 4 to 6

Preparation

For the pizza dough, place the warm water in a bowl, add the yeast, and mix. Let stand about 5 minutes until the yeast blooms. Add the lukewarm water and olive oil, and stir.

Place the flour and salt in the bowl of a stand mixer. Use the paddle attachment and mix on low. Slowly add the lukewarm water mixture until the dough forms. Use a dough hook to knead the dough until smooth, about 10 minutes. Form the dough into a ball, place in a greased bowl, and cover with plastic wrap. Let the dough rise in a warm spot until doubled in size, about 2 hours.

Punch the risen dough to deflate it, and place it on a lightly floured surface. Divide it into two equal pieces, form both into smooth balls and cover with a damp cloth. Let the dough balls rest for about 20 minutes. Preheat the oven to 500°.

Dust the pizza pan with semolina. Take one ball of dough and shape it to fit the pan. Top with the tomato sauce. Sprinkle oregano and basil over the sauce. Add mushrooms, onions and zucchini. Add a layer of sliced or shredded mozzarella over all.

Repeat with remaining dough. Bake the pizzas until the crust darkens and the cheese melts, about 8 minutes. Remove from oven and place pie-cut slices of faina on top. Return to oven for 2 minutes, no more.

Favored in Argentina, pizza a caballo *means "pizza on horseback" for the slices of seasoned flatbread called "faina" that ride on top, warmed by the melting cheese and sizzling sauce. Faina is hard to find in stores, but easy to make:*

Mix 1 cup chickpea (garbanzo) flour, ½ cup water, ½ tsp. salt, 2 Tbs. olive oil, 2 Tbs. Parmesan cheese, and black pepper in a bowl and let rest for ½ hour. Add 2 Tbs. olive oil to a baking pan and place in the oven at 450°. Add another ½ cup water to the batter, pour it in the pan and bake until crispy, about 10 minutes.

POPE BENEDICT XVI

Joseph Aloisius Ratzinger
The 265th Successor to Saint Peter
Pontifical Father from April 19, 2005 to February 28, 2013

Benedict XVI was born on April 16, 1927 in Marktl Am Inn in Bavaria, the youngest of three children. He spent his childhood in rural Bavaria. During the Nazi regime, the Ratzinger family had to endure the horrors of the war and the dreadful complications imposed on a devout Catholic family. As a young boy, like all children growing up in the Third Reich, Joseph was forced to enter the Hitler Youth. In the late days of World War II, he was pressed into service with aircraft defense forces in Munich. After the German surrender, Ratzinger was relieved to be taken into custody by American forces.

With war's end, Joseph and his brother George were finally able to join the seminary for priests at Munich and Freising. Both were welcomed to the priesthood at the Freising Cathedral in 1951. Later, George turned to a career in music as a composer and choir leader. Joseph remained committed to theological study. He became a lecturer at the archbishop's seminary, and then a professor at the University in Bonn. In 1962, he participated as an advisor to the Cardinal of Cologne at the Second Vatican Council in Rome, gaining valuable experience in the worldwide church.

Joseph Ratzinger went on to serve as professor at the Universities of Münster, Tübingen and in Regensburg, recognized as one of the leading theologians of the Church. And then came his surprising appointment as the Archbishop of Munich and Freising in 1977. In that same year, Bishop Ratzinger was elevated to Cardinal by Pope Paul VI. Appointed by Pope John Paul II to the Prefect of the Faith Congregation in Rome in 1981, Cardinal Ratzinger became one of the closest associates and most influential advisors to the Polish Pontiff. Among many important duties, he was responsible for development of the catechism of the Catholic Church. After the death of John Paul II, Cardinal Ratzinger was considered one of the most promising candidates for the papacy. On April 19, 2005, he was raised to the papal chair, selected as the 265th Successor of Saint Peter by the College of Cardinals. He took the name Benedict XVI.

In his time in papal office, Pope Benedict stressed the connection between faith and reason in countless publications, books, lectures and encyclicals. Most of all, the papal letters of Pope Benedict were heralded for the innovative theological thoughts and wisdom provided on many subjects.

When Pope Benedict made his surprise resignation announcement in February 2013, he became the first Pontiff in more than 700 years to exercise this ancient right to step down from the papacy. Today, the Pope Emeritus lives modestly, in a former monastery on the grounds of the Vatican Gardens.

We honor Pope Benedict XVI with a menu from his Bavarian homeland. Through his many years in Rome, Cardinal Ratzinger was known for frequent visits to his favorite restaurant, Cantina Tirolese, where he typically enjoyed a glass of orange-lemonade with one of his favorite Bavarian meals.

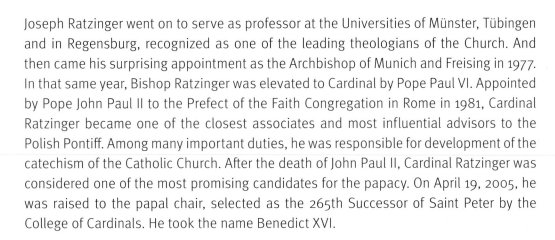

REGENSBURG SAUSAGE SALAD

Ingredients

4	Regensburg sausages (substitute Cervelat, Lyoner or similar sausages)
3	Small sweet onions, thinly sliced
3 Tbs.	White wine vinegar
3 Tbs.	Canola oil
2 Tbs.	Water
1	Small bunch of radishes, thinly sliced
4	Pickles, thinly sliced
1	Bunch of chives, finely chopped
	Sea salt
	Fresh ground black pepper

Serves 4

As Pope Benedict worked and served with great distinction for many years in Regensburg, we chose one of the famous specialties of this region as a hearty hors-d'oeuvre.

Preparation

Remove any skins from the sausages. Then, cut them into thin slices. Place the sausage slices onto four serving plates. Slice the onions into thin rings and spread over the sausages evenly.

Mix the vinegar, oil and water, and season with salt and pepper to taste. Then drizzle the dressing over the sausages and onions.

Garnish with the sliced radishes, pickles and chives, and serve.

Regensburg is known as the Weisswurst Equator, separating those in northern Germany, who typically prefer brown sausages, from those in the south who generally favor Weisswurst, or white sausage, often served at breakfast. Be sure to adhere to the rules: enjoy Weisswurst with a stein of local beer, and always consume Weisswurst before noon.

SUCKLING PIG AND DUMPLINGS

Ingredients

Suckling Pig:

2 Tbs.	Lard
4 ½ lb.	Suckling pork tenderloin
1 Tbs.	Sea salt
1 tsp.	Fresh ground black pepper
1 tsp.	Paprika
1 tsp.	Caraway seeds, crushed
1	Large Spanish onion, diced ½ inch
1	Carrot, diced ½ inch
3	Celery stalks, diced ½ inch
1	Small leek, thinly sliced
12 oz.	Dark beer

Roll Dumpling:

6	Day-old rolls or thick bread slices
½ cup	Milk
1	Small onion, minced
2 Tbs.	Butter
2 Tbs.	Flat-leaf parsley, minced
4	Eggs
	Sea salt
	Fresh ground black pepper

Serves 6 to 8

Preparation

Pre-heat the oven to 480°. Melt the lard in a frying pan over low heat. Use a carving knife to score the surface of the pork with shallow, diagonal cuts about 1 inch apart, first in one direction and then the other to create a diamond pattern. Mix the salt, pepper, paprika and caraway seeds, and then massage the mix into the meat. Put the pork in a roasting pan, cover with hot lard, and place in the oven.

Meanwhile, dice the onion, carrot and celery, and slice the leek. After the meat has cooked for 30 minutes, add the vegetables and the beer to the roasting pan. Reduce the temperature of the oven to 350°. Cook the meat for an additional 2 hours, basting occasionally with the juices.

For the dumplings, set a large pot of salted water onto boil. Heat the milk in a small saucepan over medium-low heat. Cut the bread into small pieces, place it in a bowl, and pour the heated milk over it. Peel and mince the onion. In another pan over medium heat, melt the butter and sauté the onion until translucent, about 5 minutes.

Mince the parsley, and add the parsley, onion and eggs to the bread and milk mixture. Add salt and pepper, and knead the dumpling dough well. Shape the dough into small, round dumplings. Gently drop the dumplings into the boiling water. Simmer the dumplings for about 20 minutes. Remove and drain dry.

Slice the pork, and serve with pan gravy and dumplings.

KIRSCHMICHEL

Ingredients

4	Day-old rolls or bread slices
1 ½ cups	Milk
⅓ cup	Raw cane sugar
1	Vanilla bean pod
1	Pinch of cinnamon
1 Tbs.	Lemon zest
2	Eggs
2 lbs.	Cherries, pitted
2 Tbs.	Butter
	Sea salt
	Powdered sugar

Serves 4

Preparation

Pre-heat the oven to 425°. Cut the rolls into thin slices. Mix the milk with the sugar, vanilla bean and cinnamon in a saucepan, and bring it to a boil. Then add the sliced rolls, and let stand for 10 minutes to absorb the liquid. Afterward, drain any excess milk into a separate bowl and allow it to cool. After the milk has cooled, add the eggs and lemon zest to the milk and whisk together well.

Grease 4 small, glass ramekin bowls with butter. Add a layer of bread slices, followed by a layer of the cherries, and repeat. The top layer must be the bread slices.

Fill the ramekins carefully with the milk and eggs and let rest for 30 minutes, until the bread mixture is thoroughly soaked. Place the Kirschmichel in the oven for about 30 minutes. Bake until golden brown. Before serving, sprinkle with powdered sugar.

HOLY POPE
JOHN PAUL II

Karol Józef Wojtyła
The 264th Successor of Saint Peter
Pontifical Father from October 16, 1978 to April 2, 2005

The days of his youth were not easy for Karol Józef Wojtyła.

Born in 1920 in Wadowice near Krakow in Poland, little Karol's mother died when he was 9, his older brother in 1932, then his father when he was still a boy. He said later that he "had lost everyone he loved before he was 20," yet he was unbowed by the tragedies of his youth. Strong, energetic and intellectually gifted, Wojtyła was a standout on his soccer team, in the theater as an actor and playwright, and in the classroom. In his first two years at Jagiellonian University, he learned several languages, a remarkable skill that would serve him well in years to come.

With the Nazi occupation in 1939, the university was closed and Wojtyła was forced into hard labor. In 1940, he suffered a fractured skull in one work accident, then permanent damage to his spine while working at a limestone quarry. In 1944, he was struck by a German army truck and hospitalized for weeks. He carried on.

In 1942, he joined the seminary in Krakow, attending classes in secret, in defiance of the Nazi ban. It was during these same years that Karol Wojtyła risked his own life to protect Jewish refugees, saving many lives.

Wojtyła was ordained a priest in 1946. In 1958, he was named Bishop of Krakow by Pope Pius XII and appointed Cardinal by Pope Paul VI in 1967. On October 16, 1978, Cardinal Wojtyła was selected the 264th Successor of St. Peter.

The first non-Italian pope in 455 years, Pope John Paul II set the standard for papal activism in the modern world, traveling to 104 countries, more than any other pope in history. He was outspoken in calls for reform of repressive regimes, often speaking out while he was a guest in the nations he called to account. His landmark visit to his native Poland ignited the Solidarity movement that ultimately led to freedom from communist control for Poland and much of Eastern Europe. He was a powerful force on the spiritual front as well, initiating outreach efforts to other major religions and leading the way to a new era of inter-faith communication and cooperation.

Pope John Paul II died on April 2, 2005. In 2011, he was named "blessed" by Pope Benedict and canonized to sainthood in 2014 by Pope Francis.

We pay tribute to Holy Pope John Paul II with classic recipes from his homeland, courtesy of the nuns who were summoned from Polish monasteries to care and cook for their Holy Father and remain at the Vatican today.

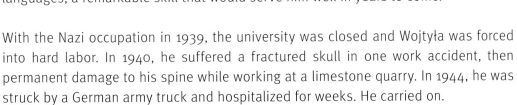

PIEROGI

Ingredients

Filling:

1	Carrot
1	Parsnip
½	Celery stalk
½	Shallot bulb
2	Bay leaves
½ lb.	Pork tenderloin
½ lb.	Chicken breast
2	Small onions, finely diced
2	Garlic cloves
3 Tbs.	Butter
	Sea salt
	Fresh ground black pepper

Pierogi Dough:

1 ½ cups	All-purpose flour
¼ cup	Water
2 Tbs.	Olive oil
1 tsp.	Sea salt

Serves 4

Preparation

Filling:

Cut all vegetables except onions into large chunks. Place the cut vegetables and bay leaves in a pot with 8 cups of water and bring to a simmer. Add the pork and chicken. Cook until tender, about 30 minutes. Drain meat and vegetables, but reserve cooking liquid. Set the meat and liquid aside, and allow it to cool. Discard the vegetables. Remove the meat and use a food processor to pulse until the meat is smooth, or chop very finely by hand. If the filling is too dry, add some of the cooking liquid. Season the meat filling with salt and pepper.

Pierogi Dough:

Set a large pot of salted water onto boil. Mix flour, water, olive oil and salt in a bowl, and knead for 10 minutes until a thick, smooth dough forms. Add more water if needed, one teaspoon at a time. Roll out the dough to about ⅛ inch. Use a cookie cutter with about a 3-inch diameter to cut out circles of the dough. Add 1 teaspoon of filling to the dough rounds and carefully fold over into half-moon shapes, pressing the edges together with your fingertips, firmly but gently. Boil the pierogi for 2 to 3 minutes, until soft. Meanwhile, finely chop the onions and garlic, then sauté them in butter over medium heat until soft, about 4 minutes. Season with salt and pepper. Mix the cooked pierogi gently with the sautéed onions and serve.

One of the darkest moments in modern times came on May 13, 1981, when Pope John Paul II was shot and critically wounded before thousands of the faithful in St. Peter's Square. Thanks to the Swiss Guard, fine doctors and nurses, and the grace of God, he survived that terrible day. It was only the beginning. Doctors cautioned that he faced a long and arduous recovery, more surgery and rehabilitation. They prescribed a very restrictive diet. The Pope made a single request: pierogi, favorite of his Polish homeland. The response was unanimous: No; out of the question. But the Pope insisted and the doctors relented. Who can say no to the Pope? Pierogi were served on a regular basis and proved to be good medicine. The Pope made a remarkable recovery, leading the Church for 24 more years as Holy Pontiff.

POLISH FLEISCHVOGEL— "BIRDS IN RED NEST"

Ingredients

Birds:

4 slices	Top round (3 oz. each)
1 ½ Tbs.	Mustard
1	Hot pepper
4	Pickles
4	Slices bacon
	Toothpicks
½ cup	All-purpose flour
4 Tbs.	Clarified butter (or oil)
½ cup	Vegetable bouillon
3 Tbs.	Heavy cream
½ Tbs.	Corn starch
	Sea salt
	Fresh ground black pepper

Red Cabbage:

1	Red cabbage, thinly sliced
4	Apples, diced ½ inch
2	Small onions, finely chopped
3	Garlic cloves
4 Tbs.	Canola oil
½ cup	Water
1 Tbs.	Honey
¼ cup	Red wine
	Sea salt
	Fresh ground black pepper

Serves 4

Preparation

Filling:

Pound the beef slices to about ¼-inch thickness. Season both sides with salt and pepper, and brush one side (the inside of the "bird") with mustard. Cut the hot peppers, pickles and bacon into strips and place on top of each beef slice. Then roll the stuffed beef into cylinders and secure with toothpicks.

Dredge each beef slice lightly with flour. Then, fry in clarified butter over medium heat, browning on all sides. Pour the bouillon into the pan and simmer on very low heat for about 1 hour. In the meantime, prepare the red cabbage.

Red cabbage:

Quarter, core and thinly slice the red cabbage. Peel and quarter the apples, and remove the seeds. Dice the apples. Mince the garlic and the onion. Sauté the onions in a pot with canola oil for a minute, then add the red cabbage, apples, garlic, water and honey to the pot. Cover and cook for 20 minutes on medium heat. Taste the cabbage and season as necessary. Then, add the red wine and simmer the cabbage again for another 15 minutes.

Take the meat out of the pan and remove the toothpicks. Add the heavy cream to the pan. Mix the corn starch in an equal amount of cold water, and add it to the cream sauce over medium heat. Stir well, and cook until desired thickness. Season the sauce with sea salt and pepper.

Serve the stuffed "birds" with pan sauce on "nests" of red cabbage.

The Swiss Chef suggests: kluski.

APPLE KUCHEN

Ingredients

Dough:

3 ½ cups	All-purpose flour
½ cup	Powdered sugar
1 tsp.	Baking powder
3 sticks	Cold butter, diced
6	Egg yolks
2 Tbs.	Sour cream

Filling:

10	Boskop (or Golden Delicious) apples, cored and thinly sliced
¼ cup	Water
2 tsp.	Cinnamon
2 Tbs.	Potato starch
3 Tbs.	Lemon juice
1 cup	Raw cane sugar

Foam:

6	Egg whites
½ cup	Raw cane sugar
2 Tbs.	Vanilla pudding mix
3 Tbs.	Breadcrumbs
	Butter for the greasing
	Powdered sugar for dusting

Serves 6 to 8

Preparation

Dough:

Place the flour, powdered sugar and baking powder into a large bowl and mix to combine. Using a pastry cutter, incorporate the diced butter until it is a coarse mix. Then, add the egg yolks and the sour cream to the dough, and mix until incorporated. Divide the dough into two parts, large and small (⅓ and ⅔). Cover with plastic wrap and place in the refrigerator for at least 4 hours to rest.

Filling:

Pre-heat oven to 350°. Peel and core the apples and cut them into thin slices. Place the apples and the water in a pot, and simmer for 15 minutes covered. Then add the cinnamon, potato starch, lemon juice and sugar. Simmer for 2 minutes. Remove the apples carefully and strain any extra liquid. Set aside to cool.

Grease a round cake pan with butter. Spread ⅔ of dough on the bottom. Bake the dough for about 8 minutes, being careful not to scorch the bottom. Remove the pan and set it aside to cool.

Foam:

Beat the egg whites, either by hand or using mixer, slowly adding the sugar. Then sprinkle in the pudding mix and whisk until foam is stiff.

To build the kuchen, on top of the pre-baked dough, add the breadcrumbs, then the egg white foam, and then the apple mixture, spreading evenly. Top with the second piece of uncooked dough.

Bake the apple cake for about 1 hour at 350° until the surface is nicely browned. Dust with powdered sugar before serving.

PERSONNEL
OF THE VATICAN

Cardinal Kurt Koch

Born in 1950 in Emmenbrücke in the Canton of Lucerne, Cardinal Koch studied theology in Munich and Lucerne, then worked as a lay theologian until 1982, when he was ordained as a priest. Starting in 1986, he was a lecturer at the Katecheti Institute in Lucerne and active as a professor at the University of Lucerne. In 1996, Koch was consecrated as bishop by Pope John Paul II, then assigned to the Basel Diocese in Switzerland.

In 2010, Pope Benedict XVI summoned Bishop Koch to Rome to work with the Ecumenical Ministry. He became an advisor to Pope Benedict on ecumenical matters and promotion of Christian unity. Later that same year, Bishop Koch was elevated to Cardinal.

As a president of the Papal Advisory Council, Cardinal Koch promotes dialogue with other churches and the Christian communities of the world, works to maintain ecumenical cooperation between the churches and Geneva, and also to deepen the dialogue with the Jewish communities.

The favorite dish of Cardinal Kurt Koch is simple, classic and modern, all at the same time: Wiener Schnitzel with French Fries.

Archbishop Georg Gänswein

Georg Gänswein was born in 1956 in Riedern, in the woods of the Black Forest, son of a blacksmith and his wife. After graduating from high school in Waldshut, he first studied in Freiburg and then went on to theological studies in Rome. In 1984, he was ordained a priest for the Diocese of Freiburg. After advanced studies at the University of Munich in Canon Law, he was called to work in Rome for the Congregation for Divine Worship and Discipline of the Sacraments in 1995. The following year, he moved to the Congregation for the Doctrine of the Faith at the request of Cardinal Ratzinger and became the Cardinal's personal secretary a year later.

With the election of Cardinal Ratzinger as Pope, Gänswein became the Personal Private Secretary of the Holy Father and moved into the Apostolic Palace, close to the Pope. In December 2012, Gänswein was named Titular Archbishop of Urbs Salvia and Prefect of the Pontifical household by Pope Benedict XVI.

After the resignation of Pope Benedict, Archbishop Gänswein remained both as Prefect and Secretary to the Pope Emeritus. As Prefect of the papal household, Gänswein is responsible for the organization of all private and public audiences, and the recordkeeping for the former Holy Father. Archbishop Gänswein coordinates the appointment calendar for the Pope Emeritus.

Cardinal Pietro Parolin

Cardinal Parolin was born at Schiavon, in the Vicenza province of northern Italy, in 1955. He entered the seminary after high school and was ordained into the priesthood in 1980. Fr. Parolin enrolled at the papal diplomat academy in Rome in 1984 and entered the diplomatic service of the Holy See in 1986, at an early age.

After extended stays in Nigeria and in Mexico, he returned to the Vatican to assume office under the Secretary of State. In 2009, Parolin was elevated to Archbishop by Pope Benedict XVI, and named Apostolic Nuncio (Ambassador of the Vatican) to Venezuela and Titular Archbishop of Aquipendium. He was appointed in 2013 by Pope Francis as Secretary of State of the Holy See, thus the virtual "Prime Minister" of the Vatican. He was elevated to Cardinal by Pope Francis in 2014.

As Secretary of State, Cardinal Parolin leads the office of the Secretariat of State of the Holy See, an authority which governs activities beyond Vatican City. The Secretary of State is responsible for political and diplomatic activities of the Holy See, which is why Cardinal Parolin is informally considered the "Number Two" of the Vatican.

Cardinal Parolin's favorite meal is Gnocchi alla Vaticano.

WIENER SCHNITZEL

Ingredients

3	Eggs
1 cup	All-purpose flour
1 cup	Fine bread crumbs
4	Veal cutlets (5 oz.)
1 stick	Butter
2	Lemons for garnishing
	Lingonberry marmalade (substitute currant jelly or cranberry marmalade, if you wish)
	Sea salt
	Fresh ground black pepper

Serves 4

Preparation

Crack the eggs in a bowl, beat them, and season with salt and pepper. Place the flour in a separate bowl, seasoning with salt and pepper, and place the fine bread crumbs into a third bowl. Pound the veal with a meat hammer to very thin, less than ¼ inch thick. Coat each piece of veal lightly in the flour. Then, dip each cutlet into the egg, and let the excess liquid drip off. Finally, coat the veal in the bread crumbs. Press the bread crumbs gently but firmly onto the meat by hand, to help the fine crumbs adhere to the coating.

Melt the stick of butter in a large frying pan over medium heat, ensuring the butter does not brown. Add the breaded veal to the pan, and cook each side for 2 to 3 minutes until golden.

Cut the lemons into slices. Remove the veal cutlets from the pan, place them on a serving plate and decorate with lemon slices. Serve with lingonberry marmalade.

The Swiss Chef says: This goes well with French Fries.

GNOCCHI AL VATICANO

Ingredients

Gnocchi:

1 ¼ lbs.	New potatoes
2	Eggs
2	Egg yolks
1 ½ cups	All-purpose flour
3 oz.	Parmesan
5 ½ Tbs.	Soft butter
1 Tbs.	Sea salt

Basil Pesto:

1 cup	Fresh basil leaves
3 Tbs.	Pine nuts, toasted
1	Garlic clove, minced
¼ cup	Grated Parmesan
⅓ cup	Olive oil
	Sea salt
	Fresh ground black pepper

Sauce:

¼ lb.	Pancetta, sliced
1	Onion, finely chopped
1	Clove of garlic, minced
½ cup	Sliced mushrooms
1	Small fennel bulb, sliced
10	Cherry tomatoes, halved
3 Tbs.	White wine
2 Tbs.	Olive oil
2 Tbs.	Butter
2 oz.	Parmesan
	Sea salt
	Fresh ground black pepper

Serves 4

Preparation

Bake and peel the potatoes the day before.

Put a large pot of salted water on to boil. Press the cooked potatoes through a ricer into a bowl. Mix in the eggs, yolks, flour, Parmesan, butter and salt. Knead into a soft dough. Turn the dough onto a flat surface. Roll it into ¾-inch-diameter sausage shapes and cut into about 1-inch-long pieces.

Boil the gnocchi until they rise to the surface. When they float, remove and rinse them under cold water. Set aside.

For the pesto, wash the basil and remove the leaves from the stems. Toast the pine nuts on low heat in a small pan with no oil for about 2 to 3 minutes, stirring often and watching carefully so they do not burn. Remove the pine nuts from the pan and cool. Mince the garlic. Pulse the basil, pine nuts and garlic in a blender or food processor until coarsely chopped. Add the Parmesan. Finally, add the olive oil, drizzling in a little at a time while blending. Season with salt and pepper to taste.

For the sauce, slice the pancetta into thin strips. Finely chop the onion, and mince the garlic. Slice the fennel and mushrooms. Halve the cherry tomatoes, and remove the seeds. Add about 2 Tbs. of olive oil to a large saucepan over medium heat. Add the onion, garlic and pancetta, and cook about 3 to 5 minutes. Add the mushrooms and the fennel, and sauté about 3 to 5 minutes. Add the white wine and the tomatoes. Remove the pan from heat, and stir in the pesto.

Place the gnocchi in a pan with 2 Tbs. of butter. Warm over low heat until the butter starts to sizzle. Mix in pesto, add sauce with pancetta and vegetables over the gnocchi. Arrange all on separate plates, sprinkle with Parmesan, and serve.

SALTIMBOCCA ALLA ROMANA

Ingredients

8	Thin veal cutlets, 3 oz. each
8	Large whole sage leaves
8	Slices prosciutto (fold once)
2 Tbs.	Butter
½ cup	Marsala wine
	Sea salt
	Fresh ground black pepper
24	Short wood toothpicks

Serves 4 to 6

Preparation

Pre-heat the oven to 180°. Season the thin veal cutlets with salt and pepper. Place one sage leaf and one slice of prosciutto on top of each cutlet, and fasten with three short toothpicks. Prepare 8 servings.

Melt the butter in a large pan over medium heat. Brown the saltimbocca in pairs, prosciutto side first, for about 1 minute. Turn and brown the veal side for another minute or two, but no more. Remove from heat as soon as veal is tender.

Remove the last saltimbocca from the pan, but save the pan with drippings to use for the sauce. Place the saltimbocca on a clean tray, and keep warm in the oven.

Keep the pan at medium heat. Add the Marsala wine to the drippings. Bring to a light boil and reduce the liquid by about half, stirring often. Season with salt and pepper to taste.

Take the saltimbocca out of the oven and place on individual plates. A bed of basil risotto is perfect for taste and display. Spoon the sauce over the top and serve. Don't forget to remove toothpicks.

The Swiss Chef suggests: basil risotto. (See BASIC RECIPES)

OFFICERS OF THE GUARD

Colonel Christoph Graf

Colonel Christoph Graf is the Commander and overall leader of the Pontifical Swiss Guard. Colonel Graf is the 35th Commander of the Guard since its foundation in 1506. The Commander is responsible for the maintenance of military discipline and readiness, enforcement of the Guard regulations and the recruitment of new members of the Guard. The Commander is the official representative of the Swiss Guard to the public at large, and to the Holy See, subject to the Holy Father and to Vatican superiors at the Office of the Secretary of State.

Christoph Graf was born in Pfaffnau in the Canton of Lucerne, and completed training at the Post Office. He entered the Pontifical Swiss Guard in 1987. Over 29 years, Graf has served as Guard Instructor, Sergeant, Sergeant-Major and Second Captain. In October 2010, he was appointed Lieutenant Colonel and Deputy Commander of the Guard. Christoph Graf was named Commander of the Pontifical Swiss Guard by Pope Francis in February 2015.

Graf is married and the father of two children. Colonel Graf's preferred meal is veal cutlets in cream sauce. We present this dish, well prepared and well intended, as sustenance and appreciation for our leader, the Commander of the Guard.

Daniel Rudolf Anrig (Commander, 2008-2015)

Daniel Anrig was born in Walenstadt in the Canton of St. Gallen. Anrig joined the Swiss Guard in 1992. In 2008, he was named Commander by Pope Benedict XVI. Colonel Anrig served with distinction at the post from 2008-2015. As Commander, Colonel Anrig was also primarily responsible for authorizing the original publication of *The Pontifical Swiss Guard — Buon Appetito*, preceding edition to *The Pontifical Swiss Guard presents The Vatican Cookbook*. We are grateful to Daniel Anrig for his years of service and for the existence of this Book.

Daniel Anrig's favorite dish is a classic Swiss original with a modern Roman twist: Cheese Torte Italiana. With respect, Anrig would like to add that his mother is chef and creator of the finest cheese torte in the world.

OFFICERS OF THE GUARD

Don Pascal Burri

The Chaplain of the Guard is responsible for the pastoral services of the guardsmen. He celebrates Holy Mass each day in our chapel, San Martino. The Chaplain organizes the annual retreat, watches over the cultural and spiritual life of the Guard, and organizes the pilgrimage trips for Guard members in Italy and across Europe, working with the Guard command. The chaplain is always available to any of the members of the Guard for counseling, guidance or assistance with any concerns.

Pascal Burri was born in Neuchâtel. After studies in history, French literature and musicology, he entered the seminary for priests at the Diocese of Geneva, Lausanne and Fribourg. After earning his degree in religious studies, Don Pascal Burri entered the priesthood in 1995. Subsequently, he worked within the diocese as pastor at different church parishes.

Since September 2014, Don Burri has been Chaplain of the Pontifical Swiss Guard. Appropriately, the favorite dish of Don Pascal Burri is lamb, in any form. Here, we present Lamb & Mediterranean Vegetables with gratitude to our Chaplain.

Major Lorenzo Merga

Major Merga is in command of the Third Squadron of the Guard. The Major is responsible for security, personnel and formal representation of the Guard. He is also responsible for administration of Italian language lessons for all Guardsmen. The musicians of our military unit, members of the Swiss Guard Military Band, are well represented in the Third Squadron.

Major Merga comes from the Canton Ticino, the Italian-speaking part of Switzerland. Before his appointment as Major, Lorenzo Merga was an instructor and Chief of Personnel for the Guard. Major Merga is married and the father of a son.

As a Ticinese, the favorite dish for Major Merga is risotto, of course.

Major Merga wears the officer uniform with helmet and feather.

Captain Frowin Bachmann

The First Captain of the Guard commands the Second Squadron which includes Guardsmen from the Romandie and Ticino districts. Apart from oversight of the squadron, the Captain is responsible as mess officer for the guard refectory and organization of the kitchen. He also provides support and coordination of media and publications, including oversight of this Book.

Bachmann comes from the rugged lands of the Canton of Schwyz. Married and the father of three, he has a decidedly Mediterranean preference for his dish: Spaghetti Frutti Di Mare.

Captain Bachmann wears the blue drill uniform, close-fit for training and drilling, and black beret, everyday headgear of the Guard.

Captain Cyrill Duruz

The Second Captain is in command of the First Squadron. Captain Duruz is responsible for Guard barracks, Officer of Materials for the armory and Officer of the Day for the swearing-in ceremony. Captain Duruz comes from the Canton of Vaud. He served with distinction as halberdier from 2000 to 2002. He has studied law at the University of Lausanne and the University of Fribourg. Cyrill Duruz was appointed in 2013 by Pope Francis as Captain of the Guard. Captain Duruz is married and father of three children. His favorite recipe is a dish from Vaud, Papet Vaudois.

Captain Duruz wears the formal uniform of the Officers of the Guard, reserved only for special occasions when Guard officers join foreign military personnel at formal events or for international ceremonies.

Sergeant Major Christian Kühne

The Sergeant Major of the Guard is responsible for personnel planning and for holiday assignments for the entire corps. The Sergeant Major is also the standard-bearer for special occasions: the Swearing-In and "Urbi et Orbi," papal benedictions at Easter and Christmas. Sergeant Major Kuhne grew up in Zurich, in the Schwamendingen district. He was trained in the office of the notary, and entered the Guard in 2006.

Sergeant Major Kuhne's Gala uniform, black with red trim and the white feather, is reserved only for the Commander and Sergeant Major.

CHEESE TORTE ITALIANA

Ingredients

Pie Crust:

1 cup	All-purpose flour
2 tsp.	Dried Italian herbs
½ tsp.	Sea salt
6 Tbs.	Cold butter, diced
6 Tbs.	Cold water

Filling:

1 ¼ cups	Whole milk
3	Eggs
1 cup	Grated Fontina
2 Tbs.	Sun-dried tomatoes, thinly sliced
1 Tbs.	Capers
⅓ cup	Gorgonzola
	Sea salt
	Fresh ground black pepper

Serves 4 to 6

Preparation

Pre-heat the oven to 425°. Mix the flour, herbs and salt in a bowl. Use a pastry cutter to blend the butter into the flour, creating a coarse, crumb-like consistency. Add the water, working quickly to bring the mixture to a thick, pliable dough without over-kneading. If the dough is too dry, add more water, half a teaspoon at a time. Roll the dough onto wax paper and cover with another sheet of wax paper. Place the dough in the refrigerator to rest, approximately 20 minutes.

In the meantime, mix the milk, eggs and grated Fontina cheese. Cut the sun-dried tomatoes into thin strips, and add them with the capers to the milk and eggs. Stir well. Season with salt and pepper to taste.

Place the dough on the bottom of a round baking dish or pie plate. Add the filling, and crumble the gorgonzola on top. Place in the oven on the lowest rack. Bake about 10 minutes, then reduce the temperature to 300° and continue baking for an additional 15 minutes.

VEAL IN CREAM SAUCE

Ingredients

1 ¼ cups	White wine
3 cups	Heavy cream
3 ½ Tbs.	Parmesan
1	Shallot, minced
1 ½ lbs.	Veal cutlets, thinly sliced
2 Tbs.	Butter
	Sea salt
	Fresh ground black pepper

Serves 4

Preparation

Make the sauce reduction one day in advance. To do so, pour the white wine into a medium saucepan and heat high enough to reduce the wine down to the consistency of light syrup. Add 2 cups of cream to the wine reduction, and reduce the mix by half again. Finally, add the Parmesan, and remove the saucepan from heat. Stir the sauce until it is thick and smooth. Lightly season the sauce with salt and pepper, and then let it cool before refrigerating overnight.

Mince the shallot. Melt the butter in a large pan over medium heat, and sauté the shallots for about 2 minutes. Then, add the sliced veal and sauté until cooked, about 3 to 5 minutes. Add the sauce reduction made the day before to the pan. Then, add the remaining cream and stir well. Continue to cook to very warm but do not boil.

Serve on individual plates. Add a small helping of chopped vegetables and herbs to each plate for a colorful flair.

The Swiss Chef suggests: lemon rice.

LAMB & MEDITERRANEAN VEGETABLES

Ingredients

Lamb loin:

1	Garlic clove, minced
4	Lamb loins, thick-sliced (about 6 oz. each)
2 Tbs.	Olive oil
1	Whole sprig rosemary
	Sea salt
	Fresh ground black pepper

Mediterranean Vegetables:

2 lbs.	Small potatoes, cut in half
4 Tbs.	Olive oil
1	Whole sprig of rosemary
1	Whole sprig of thyme
1	Mild yellow pepper, finely diced
1	Mild red pepper, finely diced
2	Zucchini, diced ½ inch
1	Eggplant, diced ½ inch
¼ cup	Cherry tomatoes, halved
	Lemon oil for sprinkling
	Sea salt
	Fresh ground black pepper

Serves 4

Preparation

Preheat the oven to 180°. Mince the garlic and set aside. Wash the lamb and dry it with a towel or paper towel. Season the meat with salt and pepper. Rub the lamb with about half of the minced garlic. Heat the olive oil in a large oven-safe pan over medium-high heat. Sear the lamb on both sides, about 4 minutes per side. Add the rosemary and remaining garlic to the pan, and place the lamb in the oven for about 30 minutes.

In the meantime, wash and halve the potatoes. Heat the olive oil in a large frying pan over medium heat. Add the potatoes, rosemary sprig and thyme sprig to the pan. Sauté the potatoes stirring occasionally until golden brown, about 15 minutes.

As the potatoes cook, dice the peppers, zucchini and eggplant, and cut the tomatoes in half. Add all of the cut vegetables to the potatoes, and cook for 3 to 5 more minutes. Season with salt and pepper to taste. Remove the pan from the heat. Discard the rosemary and thyme stems. Then, lightly drizzle the lemon oil over the vegetables while they are still very warm. Turn gently to mix.

Remove the lamb from the oven and set it aside to rest for at least 10 minutes. Add a liberal sprinkling of salt to the meat, and serve by placing the lamb on top of a bed of potatoes and vegetables.

RISOTTO AL VINO ROSSO

Ingredients

½ cup	Dried porcini mushrooms
4 cups	Vegetable bouillon
3 Tbs.	Butter
1	Scallion, finely chopped
1 cup	Arborio rice
¼ cup	Red table wine
¼ cup	Marsala wine
¼ cup	Parmesan, grated
	Sea salt
	Fresh ground black pepper

Serves 4

Preparation

Place the dried mushrooms in a bowl and add enough cold water to cover them. Allow the mushrooms to absorb the water and swell for about 30 minutes. Then, drain the mushrooms, and save the water by pouring it off into a saucepan. Add the vegetable bouillon to the mushroom water, and heat to a simmer.

Melt the butter over medium heat in a large pan. Finely chop the scallion and sauté it for 1 minute. Then, add the rice to the pan and let it toast for 1 minute, stirring often. Add the red wine and Marsala wine to the pan. Continue stirring the mix until the rice absorbs the wine. Now, add the hot vegetable bouillon to the rice one ladle at a time, over medium heat, stirring constantly. Repeat this step until you use all of the vegetable stock, and it is completely soaked in.

Add the reconstituted porcini mushrooms to the risotto, and mix. Let the mushrooms and rice cook for 5 more minutes, continuing to stir. Finally, remove the pan from heat. Sprinkle the Parmesan on the risotto. Season to taste with salt and pepper. Serve immediately.

SPAGHETTI FRUTTI DI MARE

Ingredients

1 lb.	Tomatoes, peeled and diced ½ inch
¾ lb.	Cuttlefish (or squid)
2	Onions
1 tsp.	Black peppercorns
1	Bay leaf
1 lb.	Spaghetti
4	Garlic cloves, minced
1	Pepperoncini, minced
1 ½ lbs.	Little neck clams
¾ lb.	Mussels
8	Medium-sized shrimp
½ cup	Dry white wine
2 Tbs.	Flat-leaf parsley, finely chopped
3 Tbs.	Olive oil
	Sea salt
	Fresh ground black pepper

Serves 4

Preparation

Bring a pot with 3 quarts of salted water to a low boil. Cross cut the bottom of each tomato, and blanch briefly in the hot water (about 1 to 2 minutes). Transfer the tomatoes to ice water for 1 minute to stop the cooking process. Do not discard the water; it will be used to cook the cuttlefish. Peel the tomato skins, cut into quarters, remove the seeds and dice into ½-inch pieces.

Lower the heat to bring the water to a simmer, and add the cuttlefish with one roughly chopped onion, the peppercorns and the bay leaf. Cook on simmer for about 15 minutes. Turn off the heat, and let it steep for 5 minutes more. Remove the cuttlefish from the water, set aside until cool, then cut into bite-sized strips.

Add the spaghetti to the same water and cook to *al dente*.

Meanwhile, finely chop the other onion, garlic and pepperoncini. Heat the olive oil in a large pan over medium heat. Cook the onion, garlic and pepperoncini until the onions are translucent, about 5 minutes.

Rinse the clams and mussels thoroughly. Add the clams and white wine to the saucepan and steam for about 5 minutes. Then add the mussels and shrimp, and simmer until the mussel and clam shells open, about 4 minutes. Add diced tomatoes and parsley. Remove from heat, and season to taste.

Drain the spaghetti, and mix it with the seafood sauce. Decorate with the seafood and serve on warmed plates.

PAPET VAUDOIS

Ingredients

1 ½ lbs.	Small potatoes, peeled and diced 1 inch
1	Scallion, finely chopped
2 lbs.	Leeks, finely chopped
2 Tbs.	Butter
1 cup	White wine
1 cup	Vegetable bouillon
	Grated nutmeg
4	Sausages (Cervelat or similar)
	Sea salt
	Fresh ground black pepper

Serves 4

Preparation

Peel the potatoes and cut them into large 1-inch cubes. Wash the leeks well, and finely chop the scallion and leeks. Melt the butter in a pan over low heat, and then add the leeks and scallions. Sauté for about 10 minutes until there is a good aroma. Pour in the white wine and reduce the mixture by half. Add the vegetable bouillon.

Add the potatoes to the pan, and simmer on low heat for approximately 35 minutes. Add a pinch of nutmeg, and season with salt and pepper to taste.

Meanwhile, in another pot, add the sausages and 6 cups of water. Over low heat, cook to just below a simmer. Let the sausages cook for about 35 to 40 minutes.

When both the potatoes and sausages are cooked, slice the sausages. Arrange the potato and onion hodgepodge on the plates and place the sausages prominently on top.

BRAISED LENTILS

Ingredients

¾ cup	Dried green lentils
¼ lb.	Thick-sliced bacon, diced
1	Large onion, thinly sliced
2 Tbs.	Olive oil
2 Tbs.	Butter
4 oz.	Tomato purée
4 cups	Vegetable bouillon

Serves 2 as a main course
or 4 as a side dish

Preparation

Place the lentils in a bowl, cover with cold water and refrigerate overnight (at least six hours) to soak.

Dice the bacon and thinly slice the onion. Add the olive oil and butter to a large pot over medium heat. Sauté the bacon and onions for about 5 minutes, until nicely browned.

Drain the lentils and add them to the bacon and onion. Add in the tomato purée. Pour the bouillon over the lentils, cover and cook over low heat for about 1 hour. The lentils are ready to be served, either as a side dish or a main course stew.

The Swiss Chef suggests: Add a cluster of cherry tomatoes to each bowl just before serving.

Lentils are among the oldest of common foods, a staple of many cultures across three continents for thousands of years. From Ethiopia to the Black Forest and from India to Rome, lentils have been a constant in stews and curries, soups and salads. Modern science tells us lentils are among the healthiest of foods, one of very few to retain all nutritional values through the cooking process. The Swiss Guard diet has included lentils several times a week for centuries.

LIFE IN THE SWISS GUARD

The Pontifical Swiss Guard is not only a military company, but also a community. One hundred and ten men, their wives and children live in the barracks and the facilities at the special campus for the Guard, a small Swiss homeland set aside in Vatican City. It is a unique setting for an extraordinary time in the lives of these young men.

They share long hours, intense training and sacred duties. Life in the Swiss Guard is difficult and demanding, but there are many rewards as well. The camaraderie of this elite corps of men and the spiritual energy of the Vatican enhance the experience. The wonders of the Vatican, the magic of Rome and the endless parade of visitors from every place on earth make for lasting memories.

An important addition to the Guard family is the Congregation of Albertine Sisters Serving the Poor belonging to the Franciscan family of congregations. Since 2002, these Polish Sisters have been responsible for the smooth operations in the kitchen, refectory, dining room and the Guard chapel. With much love, our Polish sisters provide family-style comforts for the young Swiss men serving far from their own homes.

THE SWISS GUARD . . . OFF DUTY

For everyone in the Guard, there is a time for duty and service, and a time to rest, relax and refresh. Many participate in the invigorating activities of arts or sports. Others seek personal experience and adventure in the rich culture and warm environment surrounding Vatican City.

Guardsmen who play an instrument can join the Guard-Internal Banda, the military band comprised of Guardsmen only that has played at countless Vatican events over many years. The Swiss Guard Band performs at the pleasure of the Pope, often including the Pontiff's birthday, always at the Swearing-In ceremony, and every December in a Christmas concert for the public in St. Peter's Square.

And then there is the FC Guardia, the Swiss Guard football team, which plays against other Vatican teams (museum employees, postal workers, technicians and the like) in intramural competition for the Vatican Cup. Combined together, they form the Vatican City National Football Team (Selezione di calcio della Città del Vaticano), the national team that proudly represents the world's smallest sovereign state in occasional international competition.

Beyond the walls of Vatican City, the Eternal City and the surrounding countryside offer abundant opportunities for further education and diversions for the members of the Guard in their spare time. The historical center of the city, the museums, the beaches in the summer, the mountains in autumn, Castel Gandolfo and the Castelli Romani with its ancient structures and lakes . . . the possibilities are endless.

POLENTA TOWERS & CHICKEN

Ingredients

Polenta:

4 cups	Chicken broth
1 cup	Coarse polenta (grits)
	Plastic wrap

Chicken:

1 lb.	Chicken, sliced (white or dark meat)
2 Tbs.	Olive oil
½ cup	White wine
¼ cup	Chicken broth
1 cup	Heavy cream
1 tsp.	Paprika
10 oz.	Mushrooms, sliced
2	Garlic cloves, minced
2 Tbs.	Flat-leaf parsley, finely chopped
	Sea salt
	Fresh ground black pepper

Serves 4

Preparation

For the polenta, bring the broth to a boil in a large pot. Pour the polenta into the boiling broth, whisking until it has thickened. Turn the heat to low, and cook another 30-40 minutes. Stir frequently. Remove from heat, and set aside to cool. Lay down a long sheet of plastic wrap on a flat surface. Pour the polenta onto the plastic wrap, and roll it in the wrap into a thick tube about 2 inches in diameter, twisting the ends to get the roll even. Place the polenta roll in the refrigerator to cool for at least 30 minutes.

Meanwhile, season the chicken with salt and pepper, and sauté it in the olive oil on high heat until cooked. Remove the chicken from the pan, and set it aside. Add the white wine and chicken broth to the pan drippings over medium heat. Let simmer until liquid is reduced by half. Lower the heat slightly and reduce the liquid by half again. Then, add the cream and paprika. Lower the heat and reduce liquid by half one more time.

Meanwhile, pre-heat the oven to 400°. Slice the mushrooms and mince the garlic. In a new pan, sauté the mushrooms and garlic over medium heat for 3 to 5 minutes. Finely chop the parsley. Remove the pan from heat. Add the parsley, and season with salt and pepper. Add the chicken to the mushrooms. Pour in the cream sauce, and mix. Keep warm.

Unwrap the polenta tube, and cut 3-inch-long "towers" from the tube. Stand the towers in a baking dish, cover with tin foil and bake for 10 minutes.

Place a polenta tower on each plate. Surround the polenta with chicken and cream sauce. Garnish with parsley, and serve.

SCALOPPINE DI VITELLO ALLA PANNA

Ingredients

2	Slices pancetta, sliced into small strips
2 Tbs.	Olive oil
4	Veal filets (about 4 oz. each)
½ tsp.	Paprika
2 Tbs.	Butter
1	Garlic clove, minced
2 Tbs.	Flat-leaf parsley, finely chopped
¾ cup	Heavy cream
	Grated nutmeg
3 oz.	Gorgonzola cheese
	Sea salt
	Fresh ground black pepper

Serves 4

Preparation

Pre-heat the oven to 175°. Slice the pancetta into small strips, and cook it with the olive oil over medium-low heat.

Meanwhile, season the veal with salt, pepper and paprika on both sides. In another pan, melt the butter over medium heat, and cook the veal until golden brown. Remove the veal from pan, place it in baking dish, and put it in the oven to keep warm.

Mince the garlic and add it to the pancetta. Finely chop the parsley. Add the parsley and the heavy cream to the pancetta. Let the mixture simmer gently, until the sauce has thickened. Add a pinch of nutmeg, and salt and pepper to taste.

Remove the veal from the oven, and turn the oven up to 425°. Spoon some of the cream sauce over each of the four filets, and top them with the Gorgonzola. Place the veal back in the oven, and bake until the cheese begins to melt.

Remove the veal from the oven, and place one filet on each plate. Top with any remaining cream sauce, and serve.

BRAISED PORK ROAST

Ingredients

1	Onion, 1-inch chunks
1	Celery stalk, 1-inch chunks
1	Carrot, 1-inch chunks
2 ½ lb.	Pork loin
3 Tbs.	Canola or vegetable oil
¾ cup	Red wine
4 cups	Veal stock (substitute beef stock if you wish)
2 Tbs.	Tomato paste
2 Tbs.	Madeira wine
1 Tbs.	Corn starch
	Sea salt
	Fresh ground black pepper

Serves 4

Preparation

Pre-heat the oven to 350°. Peel the carrot and onion. Cut the carrot, onion and celery into 1-inch chunks. Tie the pork loin with butcher's twine, and season it well with salt and pepper. In a large oven-safe pot or Dutch oven, heat the oil over medium heat, and brown the pork loin on all sides, about 1 or 2 minutes per side.

Remove the meat from the pot, and set it aside. Pour any excess oil from the pot. Return the pot to medium heat, and add the cut vegetables and the tomato paste. Cook for 3 to 5 minutes. Place the meat back in the pot. Pour in the red wine, and cook until it is reduced by about a quarter. Then, pour in the veal or beef stock until one-third of the meat is covered by the liquid.

Cover the pot, and place it in the oven until the pork reaches an internal temperature of 145° or there is just the slightest pink in the center, about an hour. Turn the meat occasionally to baste it in the liquid. Add water if needed to keep 1/3 of the pork loin covered in liquid.

As soon as the meat is tender, remove the pot from the oven. Set the meat aside to rest, and keep warm. Purée the sauce from the pot in a blender. Pour the purée through cheesecloth or a fine mesh strainer into a saucepan over medium heat. Then add the Madeira wine. Mix the corn starch with an equal amount of cold water, and gradually stir into the cooking sauce, whisking until it reaches the desired consistency. Season the sauce to taste with salt and pepper.

Slice the pork loin, cover with the sauce and serve.

The Swiss Chef suggests: porcini mushroom polenta or risotto bianco.

MONKFISH
& MONK'S BEARD GREENS

Ingredients

3	Tomatoes, peeled, dice ½ inch
2	Bunches Barba di Frate (Monk's Beard greens)
4 oz.	Pitted black olives, halved
2	Large fennel bulbs, thinly sliced
4	Monkfish filets (4 oz. each)
2 Tbs.	Olive oil
2 Tbs.	Butter
	Lemon oil for drizzling
	Sea salt
	Fresh ground black pepper

Serves 4

Preparation

Pre-heat the oven to 350°. Bring a pot with 3 quarts of salted water to a low boil. Cross cut the bottom of each tomato, and blanch briefly (about 1 to 2 minutes). Transfer the tomatoes to ice water for 1 minute to stop the cooking process. Do not discard the water; it will be used to cook the greens. Peel the tomato skins, cut into quarters, remove the seeds and dice into ½-inch pieces. Wash, trim and blanch the greens, and then place in ice water. Remove and drain.

Cut the olives in half, and cut the fennel bulb into thin slices. Season the fish with salt and pepper. Heat the olive oil in an oven-safe pan over medium heat. Sauté the fish lightly to golden brown. Bake the fish for about 4 minutes.

Heat the butter in a pan over medium heat. Sauté the fennel for 3 minutes. Add the tomatoes and olives, and cook another 2 to 3 minutes. Season to taste. Place vegetables on each plate, then a bed of greens, and arrange the fish on top. Drizzle lemon oil, and serve.

The Swiss Chef suggests: risotto bianco.

COD FISH BORGO PIO

Ingredients

3	Hot red peppers, roasted
1 Tbs.	Chili oil
1 lb.	New potatoes, peeled and sliced ⅛-inch
2	Sprigs of fresh rosemary
1	Bunch asparagus, peeled
1	Lemon
1	Sprig of fresh thyme
1 Tbs.	Coriander seeds, crushed
1 Tbs.	Fennel seeds, crushed
4	Cod filets (about 4 oz. each)
	Olive oil
	Sea salt
	Fresh ground black pepper

Serves 4

Preparation

Pre-heat the oven to 480°. Set a large pot of salted water onto boil. Cut the peppers in half, and remove the seeds and white membranes. Lay the peppers flat in a baking dish, and roast them until the skins blacken and blister. Peel the charred skin from the peppers while they are still warm. Purée the peppers with the chili oil to a coarse texture and season with sea salt and pepper.

Peel the potatoes and cut into thin slices about ⅛-inch thick. Heat about 3 Tbs. of olive oil in a pan over medium heat, add the potatoes, and season with salt. Cook to crispy brown. Near the end of the cooking time, add one sprig of rosemary.

Peel the asparagus spears, and briefly blanch them in the salted water. Immediately transfer them to ice water to stop the cooking process. Remove from the water, and drain. Heat about 2 Tbs. of olive oil in a large skillet over medium heat. Sauté the asparagus for 3 to 5 minutes. Season with salt and fresh-squeezed lemon juice.

Strip the leaves from the remaining rosemary and thyme sprigs, and finely chop the leaves. Crush the coriander and fennel seeds in a mortar. Mix the herbs and spices with a teaspoon of salt, and rub the fish filets with the mixture. Heat about 2 Tbs. of olive oil in a pan over medium heat, and sauté the cod filets lightly, about 3 minutes per side.

Arrange the crispy potatoes and hot pepper purée with the fish filets on individual plates. Garnish with the asparagus.

The Swiss Chef suggests: truffle risotto.

UNIFORM OF THE GUARD

The most famous military uniform in the world, the Swiss Guard Gala is recognized worldwide as the symbol of the ultimate guardian force, most loyal, most brave and indomitable in defense of the Holy Father in Rome.

A complex masterwork of cut and color, the uniform must be custom-made for every member of the Swiss Guard. For centuries now, tailors in residence at the Vatican barracks take minute measurements at three fittings for each new recruit, then hand cut and sew 154 fine wool cloth sections, no two alike. The entire process takes about four full days to complete. When worn, the uniform weighs only 8 pounds.

The distinctive blue, red and gold colors are derived from the crests of two distinguished families with historic ties to the Vatican, the Medicis and the Della Roveres. Swiss Guard founder, Pope Julius II, was a Della Rovere. His successor, Pope Leo X, was a Medici. The red and gold of Medici meld with the blue and gold of Della Rovere in the Swiss Guard tri-colors, with white accents at collar and cuff, black accents at shoes and beret. There have been numerous variations of clothing for special occasions, formal ceremonies and casual wear, but the Grand Gala, with few alterations, has endured as the signature uniform of the Swiss Guard.

Medici

Della Rovere

Legend has it that the Swiss Guard uniform was originally designed by Michelangelo himself, with an assist a few years later from no less than his young contemporary, Raphael.

While it is true that Michelangelo was in residence at the Vatican in formative years of the Guard (1508 to 1512), hard at work on his Sistine Chapel ceiling, and was no doubt familiar with the new company of Swiss protectors of the Pope, no hint of his involvement in the design of their uniforms has ever been found in the voluminous records, writings or art works of Michelangelo nor in the Vatican archives. It is still possible, even likely that Pope Julius II asked his favored expert in all things art to review the uniform design, but the story remains no more than legend.

The influence of his young contemporary and rival for the title of Greatest Artist of the Renaissance is beyond question. The artistry of Raphael da Urbino plays out in a symphony at the Vatican, in the Raphael Stanze at the Apostolic Palace, the tapestries of the Sistine Chapel and more. Some of his Vatican paintings include portrayals of papal guardians in brightly colored attire remarkably similar to the Grand Gala uniform of the Swiss Guard.

There is one more important credit due for the uniform of the Guard today. Jules Repond was Commander of the Guard from 1910-1921. In 1914, after painstaking research into centuries of records and the art works of Raphael and others, Commander Repond presented his personal re-design of the uniform to Vatican officials. He introduced a flat white collar to replace the pleated gorget at the throat, restored the cuirass to the original design, and added a simple Basque beret for everyday headwear. Repond's work was approved by Pope Benedict XV and implemented promptly. The Repond re-design has remained unchanged for 100 years.

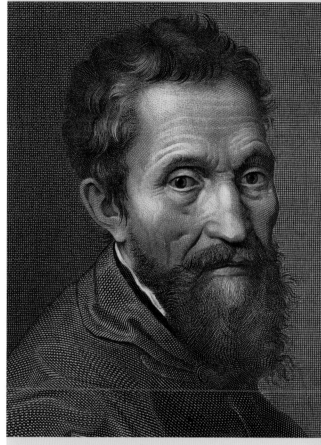

Portrait of Michelangelo Buonarra

Raphael

CHOCOLATE AMARETTO CAKE

Ingredients

9 oz.	Dark chocolate
2 sticks	Butter, diced
2 Tbs.	Amaretto
5	Egg yolks
1 cup	Raw cane sugar
3	Egg whites
1 Tbs.	Butter for greasing
	Unseasoned breadcrumbs

Serves 6 to 8

Preparation

Pre-heat the oven to 230°. Chop the chocolate coarsely, and dice the butter into pieces. Melt the chocolate with the butter in a double boiler, stirring constantly. Once the chocolate is liquefied, stir in the Amaretto.

Whisk the egg yolks with ¾ cup of the sugar in a bowl until creamy, then blend into the melted chocolate. Either by hand or using a high setting on a stand mixer or an electric hand mixer, beat the egg whites and remaining sugar until stiff peaks form, and gently fold into the chocolate mixture. Set aside about ¼ of the chocolate mix for later.

Grease a 9-inch round cake pan, and coat the bottom with a fine layer of breadcrumbs. Fill the cake pan with the chocolate mix, spreading evenly. Smooth and cover with aluminum foil. Place the cake mix in the pre-heated oven, and bake for about 20 minutes. Remove from the oven and distribute the remaining chocolate over the top. Cover again, return to oven and bake for 30 minutes more.

Cool to room temperature. When the cake is cool, remove the foil and serve slices of the cake on individual plates.

PISTACHIO TORRONE

Ingredients

5 oz.	Nougat with pistachios
2 ¼ cups	Heavy cream
2 Tbs.	Pistachio liqueur (Dumante Verdenoce)
2 oz.	Pistachios, chopped
2	Fresh figs, quartered
3 Tbs.	Pomegranate seeds

Serves 4

Preparation

Crush the nougat into small pieces in a blender. Then, either by hand or using a medium-high setting on a stand mixer or an electric hand mixer, whip the cream and the pistachio liqueur in a bowl until stiff. Add the nougat pieces to the whipped cream, and blend. Spoon the Torrone mix from the bowl and spread it into small ramekin bowls. Set the ramekins in the freezer until the Torrone is well chilled and very firm.

Chop the pistachios and cut the figs in quarters.

Before serving, dip the ramekins briefly in hot water. Set the serving plate on top of the ramekin, and turn over, tapping gently to remove the Torrone from the mold. Set each Torrone on an individual plate and garnish with the pistachios, figs and pomegranate seeds.

TIRAMISU

Ingredients

2 Tbs.	Raw cane sugar
½ cup	Espresso
2 Tbs.	Amaretto
1	Package of ladyfingers (about 7 oz.)
1 Tbs.	Cocoa powder

Cream:

4	Egg yolks, beaten
½ cup	Raw cane sugar
11 oz.	Mascarpone triple cream
	Zest of 1 lemon, grated (about 1 Tbs.)

Serves 4

Preparation

Dissolve the sugar into the espresso and allow it to cool if necessary. Then, add the Amaretto.

To make the cream, beat the egg yolks and sugar into a thick, creamy mix. Add the mascarpone and lemon zest, and mix well.

Dip the ladyfingers into the espresso, and place a layer of the ladyfingers on the bottom of a serving glass. Add a layer of cream. Alternate layers of ladyfingers and cream. The top layer should be cream.

Refrigerate for at least 6 hours before serving. Just before serving, sprinkle with cocoa powder.

PATRON SAINTS
OF THE GUARD

The first chapel of the Swiss Guard was built by order of Holy Pope Pius V in 1568 and dedicated to St. Martin and St. Sebastian. The Guardsmen have a close bond to these saints, both distinguished military officers who went on to become soldiers of Christ. Years later, St. Nicholas of Flüe, national saint of Switzerland, was added.

St. Martin of Tours

St. Martin was born the son of a tribune in the Roman Imperial Horse Guard in 316 AD in Savaria, known today as Szombathely, oldest city in Hungary. Martin served as a soldier in the Emperor's Elite Cavalry in Gaul. In 336 AD, Martin was baptized and left the army for the Church. A tireless preacher and activist for Christianity, Martin was appointed Bishop of Tours in 372 AD. He founded a monastery and led his monks in missionary work throughout the region. A venerated figure of the early Church, St. Martin became the first non-martyr elevated to sainthood. It is an honor for us to present, for our first Patron Saint, a dish *par excellance*: the Martinsgans. St. Martin's Goose is a Christmas tradition throughout much of Europe.

Saint Sebastian

Saint Sebastian was born in 250 AD in Milan to a wealthy patrician family. After a fine education, he became a captain of the Praetorian Guard, the most honored military unit of the Roman Empire. Little is known of the decision of young Sebastian to convert to Christianity.

His conversion and public activities with fellow Christians earned him the displeasure of his superiors and he was brought before the Emperor. In 288 AD, he was condemned, sentenced to execution by Nubian archers. Left for dead, his body pierced by many arrows, he was found by a pious widow and nursed back to health. He regained his health and reappeared in public to preach for Christ.

St. Sebastian is the only saint who suffered martyrdom twice. He was sentenced to death again in 304 AD, this time by flagellation, and martyred at Rome. His body was cast into the Cloaca Maxima, the sewer line of the city of Rome, but it was recovered by Christians and buried in the catacombs on the Appian Way. A church was built over his tomb in the 4th century and remains active today. For our revered St. Sebastian, we have an age-old dish from his home region in Milan: Piccata Milanese.

St. Nicholas of Flüe

Brother Klaus was born in 1417 in Flueli Sachseln in the Canton of Obwalden, Switzerland. In 1445, he married Dorothea Wyss, and together they raised a family of ten. Nicholas was a respected community leader on the local council and as a judge. He also served with distinction as a soldier in several Swiss campaigns. Yet after 1465, Nicholas withdrew more and more from public activities and committed himself to a life of prayer and fasting.

After careful consideration, and with the consent of his wife and his elder sons, he left his family and retreated to a remote place near Ranft, where he lived as a hermit and devoted all his time to prayer and fasting. In spite of his reclusive life style, Nicholas was sought out as a counselor and spiritual advisor by his Swiss countrymen, nobles and bishops, even the Emperor himself. In 1481, his wise counsel prevented war among the Swiss confederates.

In 1487, he died in holiness in Ranft. He was beatified in 1669, but was not canonized until 1947 by Pope Pius XII. Because St. Nicholas was admired for his many years of living in the most abstemious manner, at times subsisting for years only on the sustenance of Holy Communion at his daily Mass, our offered meal for him is very modest as well: a simple omelet with fresh herbs.

MARTINSGANS— ST. MARTIN'S GOOSE

Ingredients

1	Goose, about 9 lbs.
	Sea salt

Stuffing:

1 lb.	Chestnuts, shelled and steamed
1 lb.	Russet apples, cored and sliced (substitute Golden Delicious)
1	Sprig mugwort (substitute watercress leaves if you wish)

Serves 4 to 6

Preparation

Pre-heat the oven to 350°. Wash the goose and pat it dry. Rub with salt inside and out. Mix the steamed chestnuts and sliced apples with the mugwort, and stuff the goose. Lay the goose on a roasting pan, breast side down, and add about 3 inches of water. Place in the oven. After 15 minutes, prick the goose skin with a fork. After about 90 minutes, turn the goose over. Baste the goose frequently while it roasts for about 3 hours, especially in the last 30 minutes.

Roast until the skin is crispy. Then remove the goose from the oven, take it out of the roasting pan, and let it rest at least 20 minutes. Meanwhile, increase the oven temperature to 450° and return the roasting pan to the oven to let the juices brown in the oven to make gravy. Pour off the excess fat.

Carve the goose, and spoon gravy over it just before serving.

The Swiss Chef suggests: pretzel dumplings.

The legend of St. Martin says that, in the 4th century, the Christians of Tours were eager to acclaim the revered evangelist as their bishop and a crowd sought him out at the farmhouse where he had taken up residence. Reluctant to accept the honor, Martin hid in a goose pen at the farm, but a great goose began to cackle loudly, revealing his hiding place. Martin surrendered to the will of the people and agreed to his episcopal election. A tradition arose in Tours to celebrate the feast of St. Martin on November 11th with a full roasted goose, called Martinsgans, a custom still observed today in much of Central Europe.

Classic Martinsgans is prepared with mugwort, a wild herb that grows freely across Europe. The bitter and aromatic mugwort leaves are perfect with roast goose (and hardly anything else). There are substitutes: mature spinach, dandelion and collard greens can work, but genuine mugwort is best.

VEAL PICCATA MILANESE

Ingredients

Piccata:

4	Eggs, beaten
½ cup	Grated Parmesan
12 slices	Veal filet (2 oz. each)
½ cup	All-purpose flour
6 Tbs.	Clarified butter (or oil)
½ tsp.	Cayenne pepper
	Sea salt
	Fresh ground black pepper

Saffron Risotto:

4 cups	Chicken stock
3	Shallots, finely chopped
3 ½ Tbs.	Butter
1 cup	Carnaroli rice
¾ cup	White wine
0.10 oz.	Saffron threads

Serves 4 to 6

Preparation

Whisk the eggs and mix with the Parmesan. Pound the veal filets with a meat mallet to about a ¼-inch thickness. Season with salt, black pepper and cayenne, and dredge in the flour. Dip the veal in the egg and cheese mixture, and then once again in the flour. Heat the clarified butter (or oil) in a large pan over medium heat. Sauté the veal on both sides until golden brown, 1 to 2 minutes per side.

For the risotto, heat the chicken stock to a simmer in a saucepan. Peel and finely chop the shallots. In a new pan, heat 2 Tbs. of butter over medium heat, and sauté the shallots until translucent, about 3 to 5 minutes. Add the uncooked rice, stirring often to toast it for 1 to 2 minutes. Then, add the white wine. Continue to stir until the rice soaks up the wine. Add the saffron threads, and stir.

Now, add the chicken stock to the rice one ladle at a time, over medium heat, stirring constantly. Repeat this step until you use all of the chicken stock and it is completely soaked in. Add the remaining butter to the risotto and serve immediately.

Spoon risotto onto each dish, and place two or three slices of veal on top. Garnish with tomato sauce, if you wish.

SWISS OMELET WITH HERBS

Ingredients

1	Egg yolk
6	Eggs
⅓ cup	Heavy cream
3 Tbs.	Chopped herbs (such as chervil, parsley, chives or dill)
3 Tbs.	Butter
	Sea salt
	Fresh ground black pepper

Serves 1 to 2

Preparation

Whisk the egg yolk and the whole eggs together. Add the chopped herbs and the cream to the eggs, and beat until fluffy either by hand or using a medium-high setting on a stand mixer or an electric hand mixer. Season to taste with salt and pepper.

Melt half of the butter in a medium pan over low heat, and pour in the egg mixture. Stir very gently but continuously. After a minute or two, stop stirring and let the omelet set. Cook for an additional minute or two, depending on the thickness of the omelet.

Place a plate upside down on the pan, and carefully flip the omelet onto the plate. Add the remaining butter to the pan and let it melt. Then return the omelet to the pan, browned side up, sliding the omelet into the hot butter. Cook for about two more minutes. Remove the omelet from the pan when the texture is just right — this is most important for the perfect omelet — and serve immediately.

The Swiss Chef suggests: Add a dramatic garnish of whole herb leaves and sprigs just before serving.

HOLIDAYS AT THE VATICAN

The word "holiday" comes from deep Latin and Germanic roots, then on to the Old English *halig* and *dæg*, for "holy" and "day" in the 11th century, merged to encompass religious anniversaries and public festivals that include exemption from labor. There is no place that cherishes holidays more than Vatican City.

Easter is the holiest day of the year, commemorated with reverence and joy. Christmas is the happiest time for families and friends, and most exciting for children. The Urbi et Orbi blessings bestowed twice each year by His Holiness are more reasons for celebration. And when it comes to the many feast days for the saints and the exalted anniversaries of Epiphany and Assumption, Palm Sunday and Good Friday, Ascension and All Saints Day, the Vatican remembers them all.

The most important date on the Swiss Guard calendar is the Sixth of May, with the *Sacco di Roma* tribute and the Swearing-In of new recruits, a day for solemn tribute to the Stand of the Guard in 1526, when every last man gave his all in defense of the Holy Father, and a renewal of the sacred oath of the Swiss Guard to protect the Pope.

At Vatican City, Christmas time is a smorgasbord of traditions. In one apartment, it is a classic Roman holiday. In another, an Argentinian Christmas, while next door looks and sounds like Christmas in the Alps. Joy and the giving spirit are the orders of the day.

The Swiss Guard kitchen is busy with bakers and pastry chefs conjuring up cookies and cakes, delivered fresh from hot ovens to the children and parents, workers and clergy. The holiday treats are intended for all in the Vatican family

Christmas morning is very special. Each member of the Guard receives a gift from the Commander, the Chaplain and the Pope himself. These small tokens of appreciation from the Holy Father are treasured keepsakes for the Guardsmen.

When the grand ceremonies of Christmas come to an end, the men are relieved of duty and return to quarters with family and friends for an evening of Christmas gifts and sweets, music and singing. It is always a heartwarming night and a reminder of Christmas back home.

Frohe Weihnachten!
Buon Natale!
Joyeux Noel!
Merry Christmas to all!

CHOCOLATE GINGERBREAD

Ingredients

2 ½ cups	Granulated sugar
4 ½ cups	All-purpose flour
2 cups	Milk
2 ½ Tbs.	Baking powder
2 ½ tsp.	Gingerbread spices
1 tsp.	Ground ginger
¾ tsp.	Cinnamon
½ tsp.	Allspice
½ tsp.	Nutmeg
½ tsp.	Ground cloves
11 oz.	Dark chocolate

Makes 34 – 38 pieces

Preparation

Pre-heat the oven to 350°. Blend all of the ingredients except the chocolate together and mix well into a stiff dough. Cover a baking sheet with parchment paper, and evenly spread the dough on it. Place in the oven for 30 minutes. For softer gingerbread, bake less. Remove the gingerbread from the oven and set aside to cool.

In the meantime, coarsely chop the chocolate, and melt to thick syrupy consistency in a double boiler.

When the gingerbread is cool, use a large cookie cutter to cut out gingerbread in the chosen shape. Then, carefully dip the upper side of the gingerbread cakes in the melted chocolate. Place the gingerbread on wax paper to cool and set the chocolate.

Decorate in a holiday fashion.

GRITTIBÄNZE

Ingredients

4 ½ cups	All-purpose flour
1 packet	Yeast (2 ¼ tsp.)
1 tsp.	Salt
½ cup	Sugar
7 Tbs.	Butter, room temperature
1 ¼ cups	Milk, lukewarm
	Raisins for garnish
1	Egg yolk

*Makes approximately 4 pieces,
depending on size*

Preparation

Mix the flour, yeast, salt and sugar in a large bowl. Then, add the butter and the lukewarm milk to the flour mix and combine into a smooth dough. Cover with a kitchen towel and let stand in a warm spot for at least 2 hours.

Pre-heat the oven to 390°. Cut the dough into four equal-sized pieces, and then shape into chosen forms on a baking dish lined with parchment paper. Decorate with raisins for the eyes and mouth.

Brush the Grittibänze with the egg yolk, and bake for about 20 minutes, until golden brown. Depending on the thickness, the baking time may be more or less.

Let cool on a wire rack, and enjoy the Grittibänze.

Grittibänze has been a Christmas tradition for as long as the Swiss Guard has been in Rome, more than 500 years. Grittibänze means "bow-legged Benny," a playful description of the little raisin-eyed doughboy.

The sweet, brioche-style pastries are enjoyed in Swiss and German regions (and at Swiss Guard headquarters in Vatican City) throughout the holiday season, from the feast of St. Nicholas until Christmas Day.

BEEFSTEAK CAFÉ DE PARIS

Ingredients

Café de Paris butter:

7 Tbs.	Butter, room temperature
1 Tbs.	Dijon mustard
1	Egg yolk
2 Tbs.	Chopped herbs (such as Parsley, Tarragon, Rosemary)
1 Tbs.	Cognac
½ tsp.	Worcestershire sauce
1 pinch	Paprika
1 pinch	Cayenne pepper
	Sea salt
	Fresh ground black pepper
2	Carrots, peeled and cut into sticks 8 inches long
½ lb.	Snow peas
3 Tbs.	Olive oil
4	Rib eye steaks (6 to 7 oz. each)
1	Sprig of thyme
1	Garlic clove
1	Shallot, minced
1 Tbs.	Butter
½ cup	White wine
2 Tbs.	Dry white vermouth (Noilly Prat)
¾ cup	Heavy cream
¼ lb.	Bacon, diced
	Sea salt
	Fresh ground black pepper

Serves 4

Preparation

Pre-heat the oven to 175°. Place a large pot of salted water onto boil. Mix the butter with the mustard, egg yolk, chopped herbs, cognac, Worcestershire sauce, paprika and cayenne pepper until smooth. Add salt and pepper to taste. Place the butter in the refrigerator and cool to firm, at least 30 minutes.

Peel the carrots, trim the ends and cut them into sticks about 8 inches long. Blanch snow peas in the boiling water for 1 minute, then transfer to ice water. Blanch the carrots for 2 minutes, and transfer to ice water. Drain the peas and carrots, and set aside.

Season the steaks with salt and pepper. Heat the olive oil in a pan over high heat. Add the thyme and whole garlic clove to the pan. Sear the steaks on both sides for 4 minutes, and move them to a baking dish, keeping warm in the oven.

Meanwhile, make the sauce. Peel and mince the shallot, and sauté in 1 Tbs. of the butter over medium heat until translucent, about 3 minutes. Add the white wine and dry white vermouth; reduce the liquid by about one-quarter. Add the heavy cream and increase the heat. Cook until a one-third reduction in sauce.

Dice the bacon and, in a new pan, cook the bacon over high heat. When crisp, add the blanched vegetables and season with salt and pepper. After the cream sauce has reduced, whisk the cooled, solid Café de Paris butter in, stirring until it has a silky texture.

To serve, slice the steak, then add sauce to each plate. Arrange the vegetables over the sauce, and place the sliced steak on top.

The Swiss Chef suggests: rosemary hash browns.

RABBIT & ALMOND SAUCE

Ingredients

1	Onion, minced
2 Tbs.	Ground almonds
⅔ cup	Chicken broth
¼ cup	Heavy cream
1 tsp.	Thyme leaves
1 tsp.	Lemon oil
1 lb.	Filet of rabbit
½ tsp.	Cinnamon
½ tsp.	Allspice
½ lb.	French green beans
12	Small carrots, peeled
1 Tbs.	Butter
5 Tbs.	Olive oil
	Sea salt
	Fresh ground black pepper

Serves 2

Preparation

Pre-heat the oven to 175°. Set a pot of salted water onto boil. Mince the onion and sauté it with about 2 Tbs. of olive oil over medium heat until translucent. Add the ground almonds, stir briefly, pour in the broth and bring to a boil. Add the cream, the thyme and the lemon oil. Reduce the sauce by half. Season with salt and pepper. Keep warm on very low heat.

Season the rabbit filet with cinnamon, allspice, sea salt and pepper. Heat about 3 Tbs. of olive oil over medium heat, and then brown the rabbit for about 1 to 2 minutes on each side. Move the rabbit filet to a baking dish and bake for 10 minutes.

In the meantime, trim the beans and peel the carrots. Blanch the beans and carrots in the hot salted water for about 2 minutes. Then, immediately transfer to ice water to stop the cooking process. Drain. Heat the butter in a pan over medium heat, and cook the vegetables briefly. Season to taste with salt and pepper.

Remove the rabbit from the oven. Let it rest at least 10 minutes, and then slice it. To serve, spoon the almond cream sauce on each plate, add a bed of vegetables and top with the rabbit.

The Swiss Chef suggests: spicy spaetzle or saffron risotto.

SPECIAL PLACES OF THE VATICAN

The Swiss Guard knows the secrets of the Vatican.

We leave the profound diplomatic and ecclesiastic secrets to higher powers, but we know the secrets of the place itself. Vatican City is our territory. For 500 years, we have walked these halls and marched across these grounds. We have been the sentries at the walls and the keepers at the gates. We are the safeguards of the Vatican City State and all that it holds.

We know every piece of stone and marble, every patch of land. We know the secret passages and the underground vaults, the nooks and corners where history was made, the private rooms of the exalted and the well-worn paths of saints. Let us share a few of our favorite places with you.

On any given day, Vatican City welcomes more than 200,000 visitors. Flocks of the faithful, patrons of the arts, clergy and dignitaries from around the world — from dawn to dusk, the tiny nation of the Holy See is bustling with activity. In the midst of all there is a verdant island of tranquillity, the **Vatican Gardens**, a perfect place to pause, relax and enjoy the simple beauty of nature.

Is there another room on earth equal to the **Sistine Chapel**? We have witnessed the same scenes time and again. Visitors stare at the ceiling in awe, tears streaming. Others fall to their knees, overcome by the artistic splendor and the sense of divine presence in this sacred place.

The **Museums of the Vatican** pay tribute to human achievement in the arts, from the earliest days of civilization to modern times. Here are the aesthetic treasures of Ancient Egypt and the Golden Age of Greece, the glory days of Rome and the High Renaissance. Behold the masterworks of painting, marvels of sculpture, exquisite tapestries and precious creations in metal and glass, fabric and wood, jewel and stone. Swiss Guard veterans advise visitors to take a leisurely pace, pausing to fully appreciate a few selections of this peerless collection. There is not time enough to see all the wonders here.

The summer tradition of a papal retreat to **Castel Gandolfo** provides respite from the heat and a refreshing change of scenery. The Guardsmen that accompany the Pope remain on duty here, but it is a working vacation in the charm and serenity of the Alban Hills.

Of course, the centerpiece of the Vatican and the Holy See itself is **St. Peter's Basilica**. The most visited and most active church in all of Christendom is also a living museum, featuring many precious art works revered by Christians and admired by all.

The Spiral Staircase in the Pio-Clementine Museum was designed by architect Giuseppe Momo in 1932. Viewed from the ground floor, the graceful curves of the wrought iron railings, enhanced by dramatic lighting, seem to rise through the atrium skylight to the heavens above. The double helix design is actually two staircases intertwined for parallel ascent and descent, unimpeded in both directions. Inspired by the original Donato Bramante Staircase built at the far end of the same museum in 1512, Momo staircase has become a modern addition to the lofty ranks of most admired art works at the Vatican.

Designed by Baccio Pontelli at the direction of Pope Sixtus IV, the new papal chapel was built to the exact same dimensions as the Temple of Solomon, as described in Old Testament scripture. Upon its completion in 1481, Pope Sixtus summoned the leading painters of the day to provide fine art for the chapel walls. Botticelli, Rosselli, Perugino and Pinturicchio responded to the challenge with a striking array of scenes portraying the Life of Christ, Moses, Biblical scenes and a gallery of Popes.

More than 20 years later, Pope Julius II commissioned Michelangelo to paint the chapel ceiling with religious scenes to complement the wall frescos. Completed in 1512, Michelangelo's transcendent work is universally considered one of the highest achievements in art. Among the 47 distinct scenes and more than 300 characters portrayed are several iconic images that continue to influence the world of art and to inspire millions of visitors to the Vatican each year.

In 1515, Raphael added his marvelous contribution, commissioned by Pope Leo X to design and provide the art (in the form of full-sized cartoons) for 10 tapestries to adorn the lower walls.

Another generation passed before Michelangelo returned to paint the "Last Judgment" on the altar wall. The monumental (@ 40 x 45 feet) buon fresco endures as the final Sistine masterpiece.

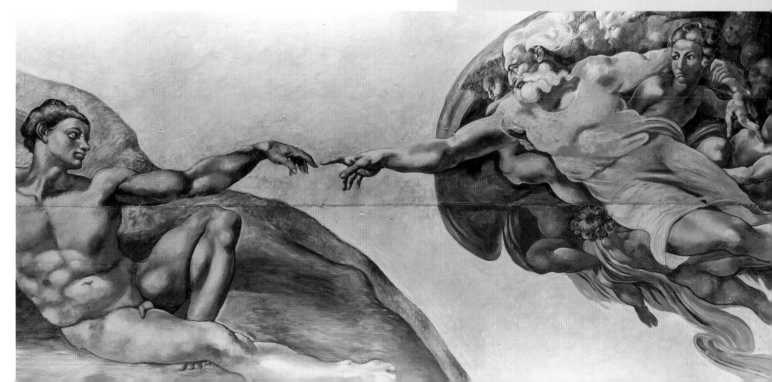

MINESTRONE

Ingredients

⅓ lb.	Dried cannellini beans
5	Tomatoes, peeled, and diced
½ lb.	Potatoes, peeled and diced
2	Carrots, peeled and diced
2	Small zucchini, diced ¼ inch
1	Small leek, thinly sliced
1	Stalk celery, thinly sliced
4 cups	Vegetable bouillon
3 Tbs.	Olive oil
1 Tbs.	Flat-leaf parsley, finely chopped
	Sea salt
	Fresh ground black pepper

Serves 4

Preparation

Cover the beans in cold water. Refrigerate overnight to soak.

On the day of preparation, cook the beans in a large pot with 3 quarts of water for about 45 minutes. Meanwhile, cross cut the bottom of each tomato, and blanch briefly in the hot water (about 1 to 2 minutes). Then, while the beans continue to cook, take the tomatoes out of the pot, and transfer them to ice water for 1 minute to stop the cooking process. Peel the tomato skins, cut into quarters, remove the seeds and dice into ½-inch pieces.

Peel the potatoes and cut into a ½-inch dice. Cut the carrots and the zucchini into a smaller ¼-inch dice. Cut the leek and the celery stalk into thin strips.

Heat the olive oil in a pot over medium heat. Add the vegetables and sauté for 5 minutes. Pour in the bouillon and cook until it is heated. Finally, add the cooked beans to the pot and heat for about 5 minutes more. Add sea salt and pepper.

Finely chop the parsley. Fill the bowls with the soup, and sprinkle the parsley on top.

TOMATO SOUP FIORENTINA

Ingredients

Tomato Soup:

1	Medium onion, minced
1 lb.	Cherry tomatoes, chopped
3 Tbs.	Olive oil
2 tsp.	Raw cane sugar
¼ cup	White balsamic vinegar
1 ½ cups	Tomato juice
1 cup	Vegetable bouillon
2 tsp.	Basil oil
	Fresh basil for garnishing
	Sea salt
	Fresh ground black pepper

Croutons:

4	Slices lightly toasted bread, cubed ½ inch
2 Tbs.	Butter
1 tsp.	Fresh rosemary, finely chopped
	Sea salt

Serves 4

Preparation

For the soup, mince the onion, chop the cherry tomatoes, and sauté in the olive oil over medium heat. Sprinkle in the sugar and let caramelize. Add the white balsamic vinegar. Pour in the tomato juice and vegetable bouillon, and let the soup simmer on low for 30 minutes.

Purée the soup in a blender to a smooth consistency, and then filter it through a fine mesh strainer or cheese cloth. Season the tomato soup with sea salt, pepper and basil oil.

For the croutons, remove the crusts from the slices of lightly toasted bread and cut into small ½-inch cubes. Melt the butter in a frying pan, and toast the bread to a golden brown. Season the croutons with salt and fresh rosemary.

Fill the soup bowls. Garnish with basil leaves and croutons.

EGGPLANT MOZZARELLA

Ingredients

1	Large eggplant, sliced 1 inch
3	Tomatoes, sliced ¾ inch
4 oz.	Mozzarella, sliced ¼ inch
¼ cup	Olive oil
1	Garlic clove, minced
1 Tbs.	Fresh thyme, finely chopped
1 Tbs.	Fresh rosemary, finely chopped
1 cup	All-purpose flour
4	Eggs, beaten
4 oz.	Grated Parmesan
3 Tbs.	Clarified butter (or oil)
	Sea salt
	Fresh ground black pepper

Serves 4 to 6

Preparation

Wash the eggplant, trim the ends off, and cut it into 8 slices each about 1 inch thick. Wash the tomatoes, and cut them into ¾-inch thick slices. Cut the mozzarella into slices, as well, about ¼-inch thick.

Finely chop the garlic, thyme and rosemary, and add it to the olive oil in a bowl. Season the olive oil with salt and pepper. Toss the eggplant slices in the oil-spice mixture to coat.

Pre-heat the oven to 480°.

Place the flour in a large bowl. In a separate large bowl, whisk the eggs and Parmesan together. Remove the eggplant slices from the seasoned olive oil, letting excess oil drip off. Coat each eggplant slice with the flour. Next, dredge the eggplant in the egg and cheese mix. Then coat the eggplant once again with the flour. Heat the clarified butter in a pan over medium heat, and fry the eggplant to a golden brown on both sides.

Place the eggplant slices in a single layer on a greased baking dish. Top each eggplant slice with the sliced tomatoes and mozzarella. Bake for about 10 minutes until the mozzarella is golden.

Simple but elegant, mozzarella cheese is the taste of summer in Italy. It can be a welcome addition to so many dishes — think of the classic Caprese. For the Swiss Guard chefs, the combination of mozzarella with eggplant or tomato begins on the working farm at Castel Gandolfo, historic summer home of the popes. Rich soil and cool air makes for lush gardens of flowers, fruits and vegetables. There is even a small herd of cows. Their milk makes our mozzarella, one of the very best. In the Guard canteen, we serve this versatile gratin one way or another, almost every day.

MUSEUMS OF THE VATICAN

The story of the Museums of the Vatican begins within days of the arrival of the Swiss Guards in Rome to begin service to the Popes, in January of 1506. An ancient marble sculpture known in antiquity as *Laocoön and His Sons* had been unearthed from a Roman vineyard. Pope Julius II came forward to purchase the magnificent work and put it on display at the Vatican, beginning a papal tradition that continues to this day. Over time, the Vatican art collection grew to a vast and varied assortment of incomparable works by the preeminent artists of all ages.

The official *Museum Christianum* was established by Pope Benedict XIV in the mid-18th century. Expansions and renovations were added at the direction of many other pontiffs. Today, the complex of museums features 54 separate galleries open to the public, attracting more than 6 million visitors each year.

Opposite page: Hundreds of incomparable paintings adorn the walls of the Vatican Museums, including the renowned works of Melozzo da Forli, an early Renaissance master whose fine linear work and innovations in perspective influenced generations of leading artists to follow, including Michelangelo and Raphael.

LASAGNA ALLA MAMMA

Ingredients

1	Batch fresh pasta dough (see Pasta Dough in Basic Recipes)
6 oz.	Ricotta
6 oz.	Grated pecorino
2	Egg yolks
1 tsp.	Basil oil
2 oz.	Pine nuts, toasted
1	Eggplant, diced ½ inch
2	Zucchini, diced ½ inch
2	Garlic cloves, minced
3 Tbs.	Olive oil
2 Tbs.	Butter, diced
	Sea salt
	Fresh ground black pepper

Serves 4 to 5

Preparation

Blend the ricotta with 4 oz. of pecorino, egg yolks, basil oil, salt and pepper to taste, and set aside. Toast the pine nuts on low heat in a small pan with no oil for 3 minutes, stirring often so they do not burn.

Boil a large pot of salted water. Pre-heat oven to 350°. Dice the eggplant and zucchini. Mince the garlic. Heat olive oil in a pan over medium heat. Add the minced garlic, diced eggplant and zucchini, and sauté 3 to 5 minutes, stirring often. When vegetables are soft, remove from heat, and let cool. Blend the vegetables with the ricotta egg mixture. Add half the pine nuts.

Roll the pasta dough into very thin sheets (a pasta machine is best). Cut the sheets into 3-inch-wide strips, then simmer in gently boiling water for 2 minutes. Remove the cooked pasta sheets and place in ice water to cool. Remove the sheets and place on a towel to dry.

Coat the pasta sheets with a thin layer of the ricotta mix. Then, roll the pasta up in tight cylinders. Set the lasagna roulades on a baking sheet and dot with the diced butter. Sprinkle the remaining pecorino over the pasta, and bake in the pre-heated oven for about 20 minutes. Set rondels on individual plates and garnish with remaining pine nuts.

One of the most notable Italian dishes, lasagna's origins are actually in Greece, where the first lasagnas were baked in clay dishes called lasanum. The Romans adopted the wide, flat pasta and added many flavorful touches to give us modern lasagna.

Lasagna Alla Mamma is a favorite with the Guard, but just whose "Mamma" provided this recipe remains a mystery. Rumor has it that Marianna, matriarch of the Roncalli family, mother of Holy Pope John XXIII and a dozen more children in a sharecropper family, is the most likely candidate. Triple all ingredients for enough lasagna to satisfy 15 hungry mouths.

CRESPELLE WITH LEEK & TRUFFLE FILLING

Ingredients

Crespelle:

¾ cup	All-purpose flour
¼ tsp.	Sea salt
1 ½ cups	Whole milk
3	Eggs
1 ½ Tbs.	Olive oil
	Olive oil for cooking

Filling:

1 lb.	Leeks, thinly sliced
½ cup	White wine
8 oz.	Ricotta
3 oz.	Grated Parmesan
2 Tbs.	Truffle oil
2 Tbs.	Olive oil
	Sea salt

Béchamel sauce:

1 Tbs.	Butter
1 Heaping Tbs.	All-purpose flour
1 cup	Whole milk
	Grated nutmeg
	Sea salt
	Fresh ground black pepper

Serves 4

Preparation

Crespelle:
Pre-heat the oven to 425°. Heat about a teaspoon of olive oil in a crepe pan (or small non-stick pan) and ladle 2 to 3 oz. of the batter into the pan per crespelle. Cook the crespelle on one side until lightly browned and then flip to cook on the other side. Cook 8 crespelle, adding more oil as necessary. Set aside and keep warm.

Filling:
Cut the leeks into thin rings and, in another pan, sauté them in about 2 Tbs. of olive oil over medium heat until they are soft, 3 to 5 minutes. Add the white wine to the pan and reduce by half. Remove the pan from heat and allow the leeks to cool slightly. Mix the cooled cooked leeks with the ricotta and 2 oz. of the Parmesan. Season the ricotta mixture with the truffle oil and sea salt to taste.

Béchamel sauce:
Heat the butter over low heat until melted. Add the flour and stir until smooth. Cook and stir to a dark blonde. Meanwhile, heat the milk in a separate pan to a high simmer. Add slowly to the butter-flour mix, whisking to very smooth. Cook over medium heat, at least 5 minutes, stirring constantly, then remove from heat. Season with salt, pepper and nutmeg, and set aside. Keep warm.

Spread the leek-ricotta mixture onto each of the cooked crespelle, and roll them up. Place the crespelle in a baking dish. Pour the Béchamel sauce over them and sprinkle the remaining Parmesan on top. Bake the crespelle until golden brown and bubbling hot on top, 12 – 15 minutes. Remove and serve promptly on individual plates.

GNOCCHI ALLA ROMANA

Ingredients

2 cups	Milk
	Grated nutmeg
½ cup	Wheat semolina flour
3	Eggs
½ cup	Grated Parmesan
7 Tbs.	Butter
	Sea salt
	Fresh ground black pepper

Serves 2 as a main course
or 4 as an appetizer or side dish

Preparation

In a saucepan, cook the milk over medium heat almost to a boil. Season with salt and pepper and a pinch of nutmeg. Add the wheat semolina flour to the hot milk and cook for 10 minutes more, stirring constantly. Then, remove the pan from the heat and set it aside to cool slightly, about 10 minutes.

Add the eggs and half of the Parmesan to the pan of milk and semolina flour, and whisk until it is a mushy mix. Pour the semolina mix onto a lightly oiled baking sheet. Spread the mixture evenly, and flatten with a spatula while still warm. Let stand for 20-25 minutes to cool.

Meanwhile, pre-heat the oven to 375°. Use a 2-inch-diameter round cookie cutter to cut round gnocchi from the cooled semolina mix. Grease a baking dish with butter, and place the gnocchi in the dish. Melt the butter in a small pot over low heat, and then pour the melted butter over each gnocchi. Sprinkle the remaining Parmesan on top. Bake the gnocchi in a pre-heated oven until golden, about 15 to 20 minutes. Do not over-bake.

Serve on individual plates garnished with springs of herbs, cherry tomatoes on the vine and roasted garlic cloves.

FETTUCCINE TRASTEVERE

Ingredients

2	Scallions, finely chopped
1	Garlic clove, minced
1	Small zucchini, sliced in strips
1	Yellow bell pepper, sliced in strips
1	Red bell pepper, sliced in strips
4 oz.	Black olives
2 oz.	Capers
2 Tbs.	Olive oil
3 Tbs.	White wine
7 oz.	Cooked white tuna
1 cup	Heavy cream
1 lb.	Fettuccine pasta
	Sea salt
	Fresh ground black pepper

Serves 4

Preparation

Set a large pot of salted water on to boil. Finely chop the scallions, and mince the garlic. Wash the zucchini and peppers, and slice them into thin strips. Set a large pot of salted water on to boil.

In the meantime, sauté the vegetables, olives and capers in the olive oil in a pan over medium heat. After 3 to 5 minutes, add the chopped scallions and minced garlic, stir well, and cook for another 5 minutes.

Pour the white wine into the pan with the vegetables. Add the tuna and the cream, and then cook until the cream is reduced by at least half. Remove from heat when you are satisfied with the texture, and season with salt and pepper.

Cook the fettuccine to *al dente*. Drain the pasta and add it to the sauce. Stir gently to mix well, and serve.

CAMPANELLE & SUN-DRIED TOMATOES

Ingredients

1	Vidalia onion, chopped fine
2 Tbs.	Olive oil
10 oz.	Sun-dried tomatoes in olive oil
4 oz.	Pitted black olives, halved
2 oz.	Capers
1 Tbs.	Chili oil
4 oz.	Sliced salami
1	Bunch arugula
1 lb.	Campanelle pasta
	Sea salt
	Fresh ground black pepper

Serves 4

Preparation

Set a large pot of salted water on to boil.

Meanwhile, finely chop the onion. Add about 2 Tbs. of olive oil to a pan over medium heat, and sauté the onions until translucent, about 3 to 5 minutes.

In a blender or food processor, purée half of the sun-dried tomatoes with olive oil, and add the purée to the sautéed onion. Cut the remaining sun-dried tomatoes into strips. Cut the black olives in half. Add the sun-dried tomato strips, olives and capers to the onions, and cook for 2 to 3 minutes. Season the sauce with sea salt, pepper and chili oil.

Quarter the slices of salami. Carefully wash and dry the fresh arugula.

Cook the campanelle pasta until al dente. Drain the pasta, and mix it with the sun-dried tomato sauce. Finally, add the salami and arugula to the hot pasta, folding in gently, and serve.

PENNE PASTA ALLA GRAPPA

Ingredients

2	Large tomatoes, quartered
1	Onion, finely chopped
1 Tbs.	Fresh basil, chopped
1 cup	Vegetable bouillon
1	Garlic clove, minced
¾ lb.	Ground beef
1 lb.	Penne pasta
3 Tbs.	Grappa
	Grated Parmesan
	Olive oil
	Sugar
	Sea salt
	Fresh ground black pepper

Béchamel Sauce:

1 Tbs.	Butter
1 Tbs.	All-purpose flour
1 cup	Milk
	Sea salt
	Fresh ground black pepper
	Grated nutmeg

Serves 4

Preparation

Quarter the tomatoes. Chop the onion. Put 2 Tbs. of olive oil in a large pot over medium heat and add half of the chopped onion, tomatoes, basil and bouillon. Simmer for 2 hours on low heat. Then, purée the tomato sauce, and strain through a sieve. Season to taste with salt, pepper and sugar.

Mince the garlic. In 2 Tbs. of olive oil in a large pot over medium heat, sauté the garlic and remaining chopped onions about 3 to 5 minutes. Add the ground beef and cook. Add the tomato sauce to the beef. Simmer on low for 30 minutes.

Meanwhile, put a large pot of salted water onto boil for the pasta. In a separate pan, melt the butter for the Béchamel sauce over low heat, and then add the flour. Mix well. Whisk in the milk while stirring constantly, and bring to a boil. Then, reduce the heat and simmer for 10 minutes while stirring. Season the sauce with salt, pepper and a pinch of nutmeg. Pour the Béchamel sauce into the tomato sauce.

Cook the penne until *al dente*. Add the cooked pasta to the sauce, and toss gently. Just before serving, add the grappa to the pasta and stir. Sprinkle with Parmesan, and serve.

Grappa is the Italian national brandy made from dregs of the wine-making process. The grape skin, seed and stem leftovers are fermented and steam-distilled according to a variety of ancient secret recipes. Like champagne, grappa is an elite and protected name, for use only in specified grappa regions of Italy and a few across the border in Switzerland.

At the Vatican, grappa is reserved for special celebrations, and is most often served as an aperitif, with or after espresso. On occasion, grappa makes a splash in the recipe, adding a sweet and tangy bite to finish the dish. But beware! Grappa can be deceptively powerful and Pope Francis himself has cautioned against over-indulgence.

CONCHIGLIONI AL FORNO

Ingredients

Conchiglioni:

2 lbs.	Fresh spinach, chopped
2	Onions, minced
3	Garlic cloves, minced
3 Tbs.	Olive oil
	Grated nutmeg
1 lb.	Ricotta
3 oz.	Mascarpone cheese
6 oz.	Grated Pecorino cheese
8	Conchiglioni
	(large sea shell pasta)
	Sea salt
	Fresh ground black pepper

Béchamel Sauce:

1 Tbs.	Butter
1 Tbs.	All-purpose flour
1 cup	Milk
	Grated nutmeg
	Sea salt
	Fresh ground black pepper

Serves 4

Preparation

Set a large pot of salted water onto boil. Pre-heat the oven to 425°.

Wash and dry the spinach, and chop it roughly. Mince the onions and garlic, and sauté them in a large pan with the olive oil. Add the spinach, and continue to sauté, stirring well, for 3 to 5 minutes. Season the vegetables with salt and pepper and a pinch of nutmeg. Drain the spinach and vegetables in a colander. Mix the ricotta, mascarpone, 4 oz. of pecorino (reserving some for garnish) and two-thirds of the cooked spinach. Stir the mix again and season with salt and pepper.

Melt the butter for the Béchamel sauce in a saucepan over low heat. Add the flour, and cook for 2 to 3 minutes, stirring often. Stir in the milk and bring to a low boil, then simmer for 10 minutes more while stirring. Season with salt, pepper and a pinch of nutmeg.

Cook the conchiglioni in salted water until al dente. Remove the pasta from the water and drain. Fill the shells with the ricotta mix.

Place the filled conchiglioni in a baking dish, and pour the Béchamel sauce over top. Sprinkle with the remaining pecorino. Place in the oven and cook until lightly golden, about 20 minutes.

To serve, briefly warm the remaining spinach and put it on the plates. Place the conchiglioni on the bed of spinach, and serve.

There are hundreds of pasta varieties in assorted shapes and sizes for countless culinary applications. Most pasta have practical, descriptive names like campanelle (little bells), stelline (tiny stars), anelli (rings), quadrefiore (square flowers), orecchiette (little ears) and farfalle (butterflies). Conchiglioni (giant shells) are the grandest of the pasta family, ranging in size from large to jumbo. For this recipe, try to find the biggest available, at least equal to a small bowl. Serve a single shell on each individual plate for a dramatic presentation.

CASTEL GANDOLFO

For centuries, the popes have spent the hot summer months at Castel Gandolfo, always accompanied by the Swiss Guard. The little town is nestled in the hills overlooking Lake Albano, the jewel of the Castelli Romani district, considered one of the most scenic and historic regions in all of Italy.

The remarkable history of the region spans 5,000 years. It is said that Alba Longia, ancient capital city of the Latin League, the first confederation of Roman villages and tribes, was built on this site in the 12th century BC by the son Aeneas himself. The legacy of Castel Gandolfo as a summer retreat dates back to the days of the luxurious villa built by Roman Emperor Domitian in the first century AD.

Today, the sprawling estate includes fine art museums, grottos, an arboretum and the Vatican Observatory. There are lush gardens that invite a stroll under the ancient trees and a working farm where fruits and vegetables thrive in the rich soil moistened by the sweet water of the lake. The tomatoes and peppers grown here are destined for Vatican kitchens, along with the finest mozzarella in Italy, courtesy of the small herd of milk cows.

While located within the town, the 110-acre property of the Apostolic Palace of Castel Gandolfo is recognized by law as part of the Vatican City State, governed by the Holy See.

FRASCATI

Frascati is a town about a dozen miles southeast of Rome, a slight detour from the road to Castel Gandolfo. Frascati is a jewel of the Alban Hills, renowned for its crisp, white Frascati wine, made from grapes cultivated in the region for 25 centuries, and as an important center of science, history and art.

In 1656 an ancient fresco was uncovered at a church in Frascati, with portraits of St. Sebastian and St. Roch, protector against plague. In the same year, a plague broke out in Rome and spread quickly across Central Italy. Only Frascati was untouched by the pestilence. Soon after, Sebastian and Roch were named twin patron saints by acclamation of the citizens of Frascati. Statues of the two saints hold prominent places in the local Cathedral of St. Peter the Apostle.

ANGUILLARA

There is a picturesque little town about 20 miles north of Rome called Anguillara Sabazia. Built around a medieval castle on the shore of Lake Bracciano, Anguillara has ancient roots that date all the way back to the Neolithic era, with remnants of a village built in the 6th Century BC.

The large crater lake is a prime drinking water reservoir for Rome and is maintained under strictest controls to insure purity; no sewage, no pollution, not even power boats are allowed. Bracciano is little known to tourists, but with the pristine water and miles of sandy beaches, it is a favorite destination of Swiss Guards for swimming, sailing and relaxing on an occasional summer day trip.

CHICKEN ARRABBIATA

Ingredients

1 ½ lbs.	Tomatoes, peeled and diced ½ inch
4	Chicken thighs
½ tsp.	Hot paprika
2	Onions, finely chopped
4	Garlic cloves, minced
2	Pepperoncini, cut into thin strips
1	Bay leaf
2	Sprigs of rosemary
2	Anchovy filets, puréed (about 1 Tbs.)
	Olive oil
	Sea salt
	Fresh ground black pepper

Serves 4

Preparation

Bring a pot with 2 quarts of salted water to a low boil. Cross cut the bottom of each tomato, and blanch briefly in the hot water (about 1 to 2 minutes). Transfer the tomatoes to ice water for 1 minute to stop the cooking process. Peel the tomato skins, cut into quarters, remove the seeds and dice into ½-inch pieces.

Season the chicken with salt, pepper and hot paprika. Add ¼ cup of olive oil to a large pan over medium-low heat, and sauté the chicken about 25 minutes with the lid on, turning often.

In the meantime, make the sauce. Finely chop the onions and mince the garlic. Heat 3 Tbs. of olive oil in a large pan, and sauté the onions and garlic until translucent, about 5 minutes. Cut the pepperoncini in half, remove the seeds, and cut into thin strips. Add the pepperoncini, diced tomatoes, bay leaf and rosemary sprigs to the pan and cook for 10 minutes on low.

Meanwhile, purée the anchovy filets with ¼ cup of water. Add the anchovy purée to the pan with the onions and pepperoncini. Simmer on low for 5 minutes. Remove the bay leaf and rosemary, and discard. Season the sauce with salt and pepper to taste. Keep the sauce on low while the chicken finishes cooking. Mix the chicken with the sauce, and serve.

The Swiss Chef suggests: parsley potatoes.

FARFALLE ALBANO

Ingredients

1 lb.	Farfalle pasta
1 lb.	Fennel, thinly sliced
2 Tbs.	Olive oil
¼ cup	White wine
2 tsp.	Grapefruit oil
12 oz.	Smoked trout filets
2 Tbs.	Fresh tarragon, chopped
¼ cup	Heavy cream
	Sea salt
	Fresh ground black pepper

Serves 4

Preparation

Set a large pot of salted water onto boil for the pasta. Cook the farfalle in the salted water until *al dente*.

In the meantime, trim off the green feathery fennel fronds, and cut the white bulb into thin slices. Heat the olive oil in a large pan over medium heat, and sauté the fennel about 5 minutes. Pour in the white wine, and bring to a simmer. Add the grapefruit oil. Cut the trout into small pieces and add to the fennel. Reduce the heat to low.

Chop the tarragon leaves finely, and add 1 Tbs. of the leaves to the sauce, reserving the other tablespoon for the garnish. Next, add the cream to the sauce and season with sea salt and pepper.

Drain the cooked farfalle, and mix the hot pasta with the sauce. Arrange on individual plates, and garnish with the remaining tarragon leaves.

RISOTTO WITH SMOKED EEL

Ingredients

3 cups	Vegetable stock
½ lb.	Smoked eel filets, diced ½ inch
⅓ lb.	Pancetta, diced ½ inch
1	Onion, minced
4 Tbs.	Butter
½ lb.	Arborio rice
½ cup	White wine
	Sea salt
	Fresh ground black pepper

Serves 4

Preparation

Heat the vegetable stock to a simmer in a saucepan.

In the meantime, dice the eel filets into ½-inch pieces. Refrigerate the eel until you are ready to serve the dish.

Dice the pancetta into ½-inch pieces, and set it aside. Mince the onion. Place 2 Tbs. of butter into a large pan over medium heat, and sauté the onion until translucent, about 5 minutes. Then, add the pancetta and cook until crisp, about 3 to 5 minutes. Add the uncooked rice, stirring to toast it lightly for 1 minute. Add the white wine. Continue stirring until the rice absorbs the wine.

Now, add the hot vegetable stock to the rice one ladle at a time, over medium heat, stirring constantly. Repeat this step until you use all of the vegetable stock, and it is completely soaked in.

When all of the stock is absorbed, remove the pan from the heat, and fold the pieces of eel into the risotto. Add the remaining butter, season to taste with salt and pepper, and serve.

FAVORITES OF ROME

Thanks to our Albertine Sisters, the food at Swiss Guard quarters is always good, healthy and hearty fare, just what we need to sustain us through long days at the Vatican.

Of course, when there is a free night or an occasional long weekend off duty, the members of the Guard are eager to move beyond the gates in search of a good meal.

What better place to seek out gastronomic adventures than the streets of Rome? The city is famous for fine restaurants featuring the many cooking styles of Italy, and the best cuisine from across the continent and beyond, with something to satisfy every palate, from elegant restaurants to corner bistros, and so many that the Guardsmen enjoy.

We cannot include them all in this Book, so we have selected just a few classic Roman recipes from two of our very favorite dining spots, La Vittoria and L'isola della Pizza.

We recommend you try them when in Rome, and if you see one of the Swiss Guards at a table, stop by to say hello.

SPAGHETTI ALLA CARBONARA

Ingredients

1 lb.	Spaghetti
½ lb.	Bacon, diced
2 Tbs.	White wine
4	Eggs, beaten
4 oz.	Grated pecorino
	Sea salt
	Fresh ground black pepper

Serves 4

Preparation

Place a pot of salted water onto boil. Cook the spaghetti in the salted water until al dente. Meanwhile, dice the bacon and cook until crisp in a large pan over medium heat. Drain off only half of the bacon grease. Add the white wine.

In a bowl, whisk the eggs, the grated pecorino cheese, pepper and salt. Set aside until the pasta is cooked.

Drain the spaghetti and add to the pan of bacon. Mix well. Remove the pan from heat. Add the egg and cheese mixture to the pan, and stir vigorously. Mix until the eggs begin to bind. Season to taste, distribute on individual plates, and serve.

HOUSE RAVIOLI

Ingredients

Ravioli Dough:

1 ½ cups	Semolina flour
3	Eggs, beaten
½ Tbs.	Olive oil
1 tsp.	Sea salt

Filling:

10 oz.	Spinach
2 Tbs.	Olive oil
11 oz.	Ricotta cheese
2 oz.	Parmesan cheese, grated
	Grated nutmeg
6 Tbs.	Butter
6	Fresh sage leaves
	Sea salt
	Fresh ground black pepper

Serves 4

Preparation

Put the semolina flour in a bowl. Whisk the eggs, salt and olive oil together, and then add the mix to the pasta flour. Knead the dough for 10 minutes until smooth, and then wrap in plastic. Place the dough in the refrigerator and let it rest for at least 6 hours.

For the filling, sauté the spinach in a pan with 2 Tbs. of olive oil until it starts to wilt. Remove the spinach from the heat and let cool. Mix the ricotta and Parmesan cheeses with the spinach, and combine well. Season with sea salt, pepper and a pinch of nutmeg. Set aside.

Place a large pot of salted water onto boil. Now, roll out the pasta dough very thinly into two large sheets, equal in size. It is best to use a pasta machine for this.

Put 1 teaspoon of the ricotta mixture about every 2 inches onto one pasta sheet. Brush a small amount of cold water around the filling to help the seams of the ravioli stick. Then cover the filling with the second pasta sheet, and press down firmly so that all of the air escapes. With a knife or a round cutter, cut the ravioli into squares, making sure the edges are tightly sealed. Boil the ravioli for about 3 to 5 minutes.

In the meantime, heat the butter in a small pan over medium-low heat, and sauté the sage leaves. Remove the ravioli from the water and drain. Then, plate the ravioli, and pour the sage butter over the top to serve.

SUPPLI—
ROMAN RICE BALLS

Ingredients

Supplì:

1 lb.	Peeled tomatoes, diced ½ inch
½	Onion, finely grated
2	Carrots, finely grated
1	Celery stalk, finely grated
2 Tbs.	Olive oil
½ lb.	Ground beef
½ cup	White wine
4 cups	Chicken broth
1 lb.	Arborio rice
5 oz.	Grated Parmesan
2	Eggs, beaten
8 oz.	Mozzarella, cubed
	Olive oil
	Sea salt
	Fresh ground black pepper

Breading:

2	Eggs, beaten
	Breadcrumbs
	Extra light olive oil or Canola oil for frying

Makes approximately 24 to 30 pieces

Preparation

Bring a pot with 2 quarts of salted water to a low boil. Cross cut the bottom of each tomato, and blanch briefly in the hot water (about 1 to 2 minutes). Transfer the tomatoes to ice water for 1 minute to stop the cooking process. Peel the tomato skins, cut into quarters, remove the seeds and dice into ½-inch pieces.

Grate the onion, carrots and celery. In a large pot, sauté the grated vegetables in 2 Tbs. of olive oil over medium heat. Add the ground beef, and brown. Deglaze with the white wine. Add the tomatoes and chicken broth. Simmer for 10 minutes.

Add the rice and simmer for an additional 20 to 30 minutes, stirring occasionally. When the rice is cooked, transfer the beef and rice mix to a bowl. Let cool, then mix in the Parmesan and beaten eggs. Stir well.

Heat the oil in a fryer or pot to 350°. Cut the mozzarella into ½-inch cubes. Take a tablespoon of the rice and form it into a ball around a mozzarella cube to make the suppli.

Beat the eggs in one bowl, and place the breadcrumbs in another bowl. To bread the balls, first dip them into the beaten egg, and then roll them in the breadcrumbs. Fry the balls until nicely browned, working in small batches. Serve immediately.

A Roman staple since the Middle Ages, the name "suppli" comes from the French word for "surprise" because of the morsel of mincemeat or cheese hidden in the center of the rice cluster coated with bread crumbs and egg, then fried to a golden brown. Handy and hearty fare, suppli was the food-on-the-run of choice for soldiers in the endless wars that raged through Italy, Europe and beyond to the Crusades to the east. In modern times, suppli morphed into a feature of antipasto and tapas dishes across the continent.

INSALATA DI GAMBERI

Ingredients

4 oz.	Dried white beans, soaked overnight
1 lb.	Fresh prawns
6 oz.	Arugula, washed and dried
1	Red onion, thinly sliced
10	Cherry tomatoes, halved
2	Lemons, juiced
⅓ cup	Olive oil
	Sea salt
	Freshly ground black pepper

Serves 2 to 3

Preparation

Cover the beans in cold water. Soak overnight.

Set a large pot of salted water onto boil. Cook the prawns in the boiling water for 3 minutes, then remove and let cool. Do not discard the water. Put the soaked beans into the same water used to cook the prawns. Let the beans simmer for about 90 minutes, then drain and let cool.

In the meantime, peel the prawns, and remove the veins. Refrigerate the prawns until you are ready to assemble the salad.

Thinly slice the onion, cut the cherry tomatoes in half, and wash and dry the arugula. Mix the arugula, tomatoes, onion, prawns and cooked beans together in a bowl.

Mix the lemon juice and olive oil together in a bowl, and drizzle over the salad. Toss to mix, season to taste, and serve.

FUSILLI ALLA CALIFFA

Ingredients

½ lb.	Roma tomatoes, peeled and diced ½ inch
1 lb.	Fusilli pasta
½ lb.	Diced bacon
10 oz.	Mushrooms, sliced
4	Basil leaves, chopped fine
1 Tbs.	Flat-leaf parsley, chopped fine
⅓ cup	Heavy cream
3 oz.	Grated pecorino
	Sea salt
	Fresh ground black pepper

Serves 4

Preparation

Bring a pot with 3 quarts of salted water to a low boil. Cross cut the tomatoes, and blanch briefly in the hot water (about 2 minutes). Transfer the tomatoes to ice water for 1 minute to stop the cooking process. Set aside the water for cooking the pasta. Peel the tomato skins, cut into quarters, remove the seeds and dice into ½-inch pieces. Add the pasta to the water and cook until *al dente*.

Meanwhile, place the bacon in a large pan, and sauté it over medium heat until crisp, about 5 minutes. Clean and slice the mushrooms. Finely chop the parsley and basil. Add the mushrooms, parsley and basil to the bacon, and sauté for 5 minutes. Add the diced tomatoes, and continue to cook on low heat for 2 minutes. Season to taste.

Drain pasta and add to pan with bacon and mushrooms. Pour in heavy cream, and cook for about 1 minute more. Sprinkle with pecorino cheese, and serve.

RISOTTO & ARTICHOKES

Ingredients

12	Small Italian artichokes, trimmed and diced ½ inch
4 cups	Vegetable stock
3	Shallots, minced
2 Tbs.	Butter
¾ cup	Arborio rice
¾ cup	White wine
¼ cup	Heavy cream
2 Tbs.	Fresh lemon juice
	Sea salt
	Fresh ground black pepper

Serves 4

Preparation

Remove the tough outer leaves from the artichokes until you see leaves that are pale yellow at the bottom. Cut off the stem, and peel any rough skin around the stem. Trim about ½ inch off of the top of the artichoke. Cut the artichokes in half, and remove any fuzz from the center. Baby or young artichokes may not have any fuzz, but larger artichokes likely will; be careful to remove it all. Quarter the cleaned artichokes and soak in water with lemon juice to prevent browning.

Heat the vegetable stock to a simmer in a saucepan. Meanwhile, peel and mince the shallots. In another large pan, heat the butter, and sauté the shallots over medium heat until translucent, about 3 minutes. Drain the artichoke hearts, dice into ½-inch pieces, and add to the shallots.

Add the uncooked rice to the pan with the shallots and artichokes. Stir briefly to toast the rice, and then pour in the white wine. Continue stirring the mix until the rice absorbs the wine. Now, add the hot vegetable stock to the rice one ladle at a time, over medium heat, stirring constantly. Repeat this step until you use all of the vegetable stock, and it is completely soaked in.

After all of the stock has been absorbed, add the heavy cream to the pan, cover, turn off the heat, and let the risotto rest for about 5 minutes. Stir again, season to taste, and serve immediately.

BASIC RECIPES

PASTA DOUGH

Ingredients

1 ¼ cup	Semolina flour
3	Eggs
1 tsp.	Sea salt
0.10 oz.	Saffron threads
1 Tbs.	Olive oil

Serves 4

Put the pasta flour in a bowl. In another bowl, mix the eggs, salt, saffron and olive oil together. Then add the egg mixture to the semolina flour, and combine to form a firm dough. Knead the dough for several minutes. Wrap the dough in plastic film and let rest in the refrigerator for at least 6 hours. Roll the dough according to the specific recipe's directions.

PIZZA DOUGH

Ingredients

½ cup	Water, about 110°
1	Yeast packet (2 ¼ tsp.)
4 cups	Bread flour, plus more for dusting
2 Tbs.	Olive oil
1 ½ tsp.	Sea salt
	Olive oil for greasing

Serves 6 to 8

Mix warm water and yeast. Let stand about 5 minutes. In a large bowl, mix 4 cups of bread flour, salt, oil and yeast mix. Slowly add the lukewarm water until dough forms. Knead until the dough is smooth, about 10 minutes. Form dough into a ball, place in an oiled bowl, and cover with plastic wrap. Let rise in a warm spot until doubled in size, about 2 hours. Punch the risen dough to deflate it, and place on a lightly floured surface. Divide into two equal pieces, form both into smooth balls and cover with a damp cloth. Let rest about 20 minutes. Preheat oven to 500° and top pizza as desired. Bake about 10 minutes.

BREAD DUMPLINGS

Ingredients

6	Day-old dinner rolls or thick slices of bread
½	Cup of milk
1	Onion, minced
2 Tbs.	Butter
1	Small bunch parsley, minced
4	Eggs
	Sea salt
	Freshly ground black pepper

Serves 2 to 4

Set a large pot of salted water onto boil. Heat the milk in a small saucepan. Cut the bread into small pieces, place it in a bowl, and pour the milk over it. Peel and mince the onion. Sauté it in 2 Tbs. of butter about 5 minutes. Mince the parsley. Add the parsley, onion and eggs to the bread and milk. Add salt and pepper, and knead the dumpling dough well. Shape the dough into small, round dumplings. Gently drop the dumplings into the boiling water, and simmer for about 20 minutes.

PRETZEL DUMPLINGS

Ingredients

6	Day-old soft pretzels
½ cup	Milk
1	Onion, minced
2 Tbs.	Butter
1	Small bunch parsley, minced
4	Eggs
	Sea salt
	Fresh ground black pepper

Set a large pot of salted water onto boil. Heat the milk in a small saucepan. Cut the pretzels into small pieces, place them in a bowl, and pour the milk over them. Peel and mince the onion. Sauté it in 2 Tbs. butter about 5 minutes. Mince the parsley. Add the parsley, onion and eggs to the pretzels and milk. Add salt and pepper, and knead the dough well. Shape the dough into small, round dumplings. Gently drop the dumplings into the boiling water for about 20 minutes.

Serves 2 to 4

LEMON RICE

Ingredients

1 Tbs.	Olive oil
¾ cup	White rice
½ cup	Orange juice
	Zest of 1 lemon, about 1 Tbs.
3 cups	Water
	Sea salt

Heat the olive oil in a large saucepan over medium heat. Add the rice and stir, toasting for about 1 minute. Add the orange juice and the zest of one lemon. Stir, add the water and about a teaspoon of salt. Bring to a boil, cover and simmer for about 20 minutes. Season with salt to taste, and serve.

Serves 4

POTATO BUTTERNUT SQUASH PURÉE

Ingredients

1 lb.	Butternut squash
¾ lb.	Potatoes
⅓ cup	Milk
4 Tbs.	Butter
⅓ cup	Heavy cream
2 oz.	Grated Parmesan
	Ground nutmeg
	Sea salt
	Fresh ground black pepper

Place a large pot of salted water onto boil. Peel and cut the squash and potatoes into large pieces. Place the vegetables in the boiling water and cook until soft. Drain, and let stand for about 10 minutes to cool. Meanwhile, heat the milk, butter and cream to a low simmer in the pot. Press the cooked potato and squash through a potato ricer into the pot of milk. Stir vigorously with a whisk until creamy. Season with Parmesan, a pinch of nutmeg, salt and pepper.

Serves 4 to 6

ROSEMARY HASH BROWNS

Ingredients

2 lbs.	Potatoes
4 Tbs.	Butter
1 Tbs.	Rosemary leaves, chopped
	Sea salt
	Fresh ground black pepper

Serves 4 to 6

Boil the potatoes until soft, and let the cooked potatoes chill for at least 4 hours, preferably a day. Peel and grate the cooked potatoes into a bowl. Season with sea salt and pepper. Add rosemary leaves and mix well. Melt the butter in a large pan over medium heat and add the potatoes. Let the potatoes cook until a golden brown crust forms. Flip over and cook the other side to golden brown.

POTATOES AU GRATIN

Ingredients

2 lbs.	Potatoes
1 ½ cups	Heavy cream
¾ cup	Milk
3 Tbs.	Butter
1	Garlic clove, minced
	Butter for greasing
	Sea salt

Serves 6 to 8

Pre-heat the oven to 350°. Peel, wash and cut the potatoes into very thin slices. Heat the heavy cream, milk and butter in a small pan. Mince the garlic, and add it to the cream. Season the cream with salt. Grease the baking dish with butter. Layer the potato slices in the baking dish. Pour the cream sauce evenly over the potatoes. Bake covered for about 1 hour, then uncover and bake another 30 minutes until tender.

KLUSKI

Ingredients

2 lbs.	Potatoes, boiled
1 cup	Potato flour (approximately)
1	Egg
	Sea salt

Serves 6

Cook the potatoes in salted water until the skin is soft. Remove the potatoes, but do not discard the water. Peel the potatoes while still warm, then set aside to cool. Push the potatoes through a ricer into a bowl. Add the potato flour, and mix until combined. Add the egg and some sea salt. Mix into a dough, adding more flour if necessary, and knead well. Hand form about 1 Tbs. of dough into balls. Press the balls on a flat surface into thin, round circles, about ½-inch thick. Make a small indentation in each circle with your finger. Slip the kluski into boiling water in small batches. After they rise to the surface, continue to boil for about a minute, and then lift them from the water with a slotted spoon and serve immediately.

FRENCH FRIED POTATOES

Ingredients

1 ½ lbs.	Potatoes
	Oil for frying
	Sea salt

Serves 4

Pre-heat the oil in a deep fryer or a large pot to 350°. Wash and peel the potatoes, and cut them into long, thin, uniform sticks. Rinse the potato sticks, and dry them thoroughly on a thick kitchen towel. Fry the potatoes until golden and crispy. Remove the potatoes, and drain on paper towels. Salt the fried potatoes well, and serve in bowl with paper towels on the bottom.

PARSLEY POTATOES

Ingredients

2 lbs.	Potatoes, par-cooked
2 Tbs.	Butter
3 Tbs.	Olive oil
1	Small bunch Parsley, minced
2	Garlic cloves, minced
	Sea salt

Serves 6

Cook the potatoes for about 15 minutes in boiling water. Drain and set aside to cool. Then peel the potatoes and cut them into thick slices, about ½ inch. Heat the butter and olive oil in large pan over medium heat. Add the potatoes and season with sea salt, and cook until crispy, about 10 to 15 minutes. Mince the parsley and garlic, and add both to the pan. Sauté about 3 minutes, and then serve.

HOUSE POTATOES

Ingredients

2 lbs.	New potatoes
2	Large onions
1	Mild yellow pepper
2	Mild red pepper
1	Zucchini
6	Garlic cloves, quartered
¼ cup	Olive oil
2 Tbs.	Capers in oil
½ Tbs.	Fresh rosemary
4 oz.	Pitted black olives
	Sea salt/Fresh black pepper

Serves 6 to 8

Pre-heat the oven to 425°. Wash and halve the potatoes. Peel the onions, remove the core from the peppers and trim the zucchini ends. Cut the onions, peppers and zucchini into 1-inch chunks. Peel and quarter the garlic cloves. Put the potatoes, vegetables and garlic in a baking dish. Season generously with salt and pepper. Mix in the oil, capers, rosemary and olives. Place the dish in the preheated oven for about 45 minutes until the potatoes are tender, and serve.

RISOTTO BIANCO

Ingredients

4 cups	Vegetable stock
3	Shallots, minced
4 Tbs.	Butter
¾ cup	Arborio rice
¾ cup	White wine
½ cup	Heavy cream
2 Tbs.	Grated Parmesan

Serves 4

Heat the vegetable stock to a simmer in a saucepan. Meanwhile, peel and mince the shallots. Sauté them in 2 Tbs. butter for about 3 minutes. Add the uncooked rice, stirring to toast it lightly for 1 minute. Add the white wine. Continue stirring until the rice absorbs the wine. Add the hot vegetable stock to the rice one ladle at a time, over medium heat, stirring constantly. Repeat this step until you use all of the vegetable stock, and it is completely soaked in. Add the heavy cream and the remaining butter. Stir, cover and let rest for 5 minutes. Add the Parmesan and salt to taste. Stir again, and serve.

TRUFFLE RISOTTO

Ingredients

4 cups	Chicken stock
3	Shallots, minced
2 Tbs.	Olive oil
¾ cup	Arborio rice
¾ cup	White wine
½ cup	Heavy cream
3 Tbs.	Truffle oil
	Sea salt

Serves 4

Heat the chicken stock to a simmer in a saucepan. Meanwhile, peel and mince the shallots. Sauté them in 2 Tbs. olive oil for about 3 minutes. Add the uncooked rice, stirring to toast it lightly for 1 minute. Add the white wine. Continue stirring until the rice absorbs the wine. Add the hot chicken stock to the rice one ladle at a time, over medium heat, stirring constantly. Repeat this step until you use all of the chicken stock, and it is completely soaked in. Add the heavy cream and the truffle oil. Stir, cover and let rest for 5 minutes. Add salt to taste, stir again, and serve.

BASIL RISOTTO

Ingredients

4 cups	Vegetable stock
3	Shallots, minced
2 Tbs.	Butter
¾ cup	Arborio rice
3 cups	White wine
½ cup	Heavy cream
2 Tbs.	Grated Parmesan
3 Tbs.	Basil pesto
	Sea salt

Serves 4

Heat the vegetable stock to a simmer in a saucepan. Meanwhile, peel and mince the shallots. Sauté them in 2 Tbs. butter for about 3 minutes. Add the uncooked rice, stirring to toast it lightly for 1 minute. Add the white wine. Continue stirring until the rice absorbs the wine. Add the hot vegetable stock to the rice one ladle at a time, over medium heat, stirring constantly. Repeat this step until you use all of the vegetable stock, and it is completely soaked in. Add the heavy cream. Stir, cover and let rest for 5 minutes. Add the Parmesan, basil pesto and salt to taste. Stir again, and serve.

SPAETZLE

Ingredients

1 cup	All-purpose flour
3	Eggs, beaten
⅓ cup	Milk
	Ground nutmeg
	Sea salt
2 Tbs.	Butter

Serves 4

Set a large pot of salted water onto boil. Mix the flour and eggs in a bowl. Add the milk gradually until the dough comes together. Season with salt and grated nutmeg. Press the dough through a noodle sieve into the boiling water. Or, if you wish, push the dough through a colander or slotted spoon. When the Spaetzle rises to the surface, remove from the water. Transfer to a colander. Rinse with cold water. Drain. Melt the butter in a pan over medium heat, and sauté the Spaetzle briefly, adding spices just before serving.

SPICY SPAETZLE

Ingredients

1 cup	All-purpose flour
3	Eggs
½ cup	Milk
½ Tbs.	Sea salt
2 pinches	Ground cinnamon
1 pinch	Ground cardamom
1 pinch	Ground allspice
1 pinch	Ground nutmeg
2 Tbs.	Butter

Serves 4

Set a large pot of salted water onto boil. Mix the flour and eggs in a bowl. Add the milk gradually until the dough comes together. Add the salt and spices. Press the dough through a Spaetzle ricer into the boiling water. Or, if you wish, push the dough through a colander or slotted spoon. When the Spaetzle rises to the surface, remove from the water. Transfer to a colander. Rinse with cold water. Drain. Melt the butter in a pan over medium heat, and sauté the Spaetzle briefly, adding spices just before serving.

MUSHROOM POLENTA

Ingredients

10 oz.	Mushrooms, sliced
2	Garlic cloves, minced
3 Tbs.	Olive oil
1 cup	Cornmeal (grits)
2 cups	Vegetable stock
2 cups	Milk
1 Tbs.	Parsley, chopped
	Sea salt

Serves 4

Clean the mushrooms and cut them into thin slices. Peel and mince the garlic cloves. Heat the olive oil in a large pot over medium heat, and sauté the garlic about 2 minutes. Add the mushrooms and salt, and sauté for 5 minutes. Pour in the vegetable stock and milk, and bring to a boil. Stir in the cornmeal, and simmer for 10 minutes, stirring often. Add the chopped parsley and salt to taste just before serving.

TABLE PRAYERS

The grace before meals is an expression of gratitude to God for the food before us. It is a thanksgiving as well, to all those involved in the preparation of the meal, from the farmer in the field to the cook in the kitchen, so many hands and so much work to bring us our daily bread.

We must also remember all who are not as blessed, who rarely have a full meal and must go hungry day after day. The pause before eating is a time for deep appreciation of our own food, and compassion for so many others, caught up in crises of war, drought, famine and disaster, deprived of sustenance and the simple pleasure of food. We pray for an end to the plague of hunger for all our brothers and sisters in the world.

Classic

O God, from Whom we receive everything,
We give thanks to You for these gifts.
You provide us with our daily bread because You love us so.
We ask You to bless what You set before us!
Amen

Come, Lord Jesus, be our guest
And bless what You have graciously given us.
Amen

To You, O God, for food and drink, we give all praise and thanks.
You give us today, You will give us tomorrow.
We praise You for all of our lives.
Amen

Children

Every little animal has food to eat, Each little flower takes a sip of water from You.
Let me never forget, Dear God, I must thank You!
All these good gifts, Everything we have, Comes from You, O God.
Thank You for all!
Amen

Latin

Oculi omnium in te sperant, Domine, et tu das escam illorum in tempore opportune:
Aperis tu manum tuam, et imples omne animal benedictione.

The eyes of all look to Thee in hope, O Lord: and Thou givest them sustenance in due season.
Open Thy hand, and bestow Thy blessing to fulfill the needs of every living thing.

IN·FLAGELLA
PARATVS·SVM

A NOTE OF THANKS

There were so many valuable contributors to the creation of this Book that we cannot thank them all, but we must acknowledge the special contributions of the following:

The Holy See of the Vatican City State

Seàn Cardinal O'Malley

The Pontifical Swiss Guard

Commander Christoph Graf

Captain Frowin Bachmann

Werd & Weber Verlag AG

Annette Weber

Archangel Productions USA

Katharina Anna Dunigan

Sandra Sullivan

Michael Heaton

Michael Antonello

Michael Criscione

Anne Sheehan Kelly

Richard Morris

Langenthal China Company

Nica, Felix and Benjamin Geisser

A great big thank you to All

And God bless!

ABOUT THE AUTHORS

David Geisser

David Geisser spent his youth in the Wetzikon district of Zurich and created his first cookbook at the age of 18. A school term paper became *80 Recipes Around the World*, a sensation in the Swiss media that launched his culinary career. At 20, he co-authored another best seller, *Through the Seasons*, with grand chef Stephan Wunderlich. Hailed as a chef and author of extraordinary talent, Geisser joined the Swiss Guard in 2013 to take a leading role in the creation of *Pontifical Swiss Guard presents The Vatican Cookbook*.

Erwin Niederberger

Erwin Niederberger was born in Lucerne and raised in Kussnacht am Rigi, Switzerland. An accomplished pastry chef, Niederberger entered the Guard in 1999, serving for many years as Sergeant of the Guard and Chief Information Officer. The narrative and historical passages and editorial supervision of this Book are primarily thanks to Erwin Niederberger.

Daniel Anrig

Born in Walenstadt in the Canton of St. Gallen, Daniel Anrig joined the Swiss Guard in 1992 and served with honor and distinction. Commander of the Guard from 2008-2015, Anrig was responsible for the authorization and publication of *Pontifical Swiss Guard — Buon Appetito*, predecessor to and inspiration for this Book.

Thomas Kelly

Thomas Kelly is a writer, author and editor from Cleveland, Ohio, USA. Kelly provided new text and other new content, and acted as Supervising Editor for the supplements and modifications to the revised version of *Pontifical Swiss Guard — Buon Appetito*, published in North America as *Pontifical Swiss Guard presents The Vatican Cookbook*.

PHOTOGRAPHY END NOTES

Pope Benedict XVI and Swiss Guards at Mass (8)
Pope Benedict in a pastoral moment with two Swiss Guards at Mass in St. Peter's Basilica, with the famed statue of *St. Veronica of the Veil* by Francesco Mochi looming above. The image conveys both grandeur and intimacy with superb balance. (Grzegorz Galazka)

Holy Pope John Paul II (10)
A defining informal portrait of Holy Pope John Paul II evinces the strength, benevolence and wisdom of the longest-serving and most beloved Pope of modern times. (Grzegorz Galazka)

Pope Francis & Company of the Swiss Guard (24-25)
Pope Francis and his Swiss Guards pose in Clementine Hall of the Apostolic Palace, beneath the 16th century fresco, "The Baptism of St. Clement" by Cherubino Alberti and Baldassare Croce. The pride of the Guard in the presence of His Holiness, and the elegance of the grand hall, host to 48 Popes and hundreds of world dignitaries, are on full display. (Katarzyna Artymiak)

Pope Francis leads Easter Mass at St. Peter's Basilica (124-125)
A panoramic view capturing the majesty of the interior of St. Peter's Basilica at Solemn High Mass on Easter, 2013, with Pope Francis leading the faithful in the celebration. (Giulio Napolitano)

Swiss Guard at the Sistine Chapel (140-141)
The abundance and complexity of the art on the ceiling of the Sistine Chapel is beyond capturing in a single photograph. Here, careful composition with the Swiss Guardsman as a foreground anchor provides the ideal framework for the presentation of Michelangelo's masterpiece. (Katarzyna Artymiak)

Gallery Ceiling at the Vatican Museums (150-151)
The Gallery of Maps was commissioned by Pope Gregory XIII in 1580 as part of the first vast expansion of the Vatican Museums. The stunning *trompe l'oeil* decorations and paintings that cover the full 120-meter length of the vaulted ceiling are the work of a team of Mannerist artists led by Cesare Nebbia and Girolamo Muziano. (S-F)

Cathedra Petri and the Gold Window (156-157)
The Cathedra Petri (Chair of Saint Peter) is an ancient wooden relic revered as the chair of Apostle Peter himself, enshrined in a gilt bronze casing by Gian Lorenzo Bernini in the mid-17th century. Behind and above the Cathedra, a blaze of light through the stained glass illuminates the Dove of the Holy Spirit, flanked by a chorus of alabaster angels, the entire scene framed with towering pilasters designed by Michelangelo. This is the "Gold Window." (Anilah)

St. Michael the Archangel (164-165)
The massive mausoleum of the Roman emperor Hadrian was built in 139 AD, tallest edifice in Rome at the time. Acquired by the Church centuries later, it was converted to a castle and fortress. Legend holds that the Archangel Michael appeared atop the structure sheathing his sword as a sign of the end of the plague of 590 AD. In 1536, Raphael da Montelupo created this marble statue of Saint Michael to surmount the rechristened Castel Sant'Angelo.

PHOTOGRAPH CREDITS

The photography is fundamental to the character and quality of this Book, and we owe our thanks to the twin sisters, Katarzyna and Anna Artymiak, photographic artist and coordinator for this project. All photos in this Book are by Katarzyna Artymiak, except as noted below.

ADDITIONAL PHOTOGRAPHS BY:

Grzegorz Galazka	Holy Pope John Paul II (5), Pope Benedict XVI & Swiss Guard (8), Holy Pope John Paul II (10), Holy Pope John Paul II (52)
Frowin Bachmann	Commandant Christoph Graf (9)
Lapas	St. Peter's Basilica Dome (22)
Fabio Montagna, Milan	Daniel Anrig (27), Daniel Anrig (199)
Giulio Napolitano	Pope Francis Greets Bishops at St. Peter's (32), Pope Francis and Children (33), Easter Mass at St. Peter's (124-125), Pope Francis/Crowd (28-29), Smiling Pope Francis (42), Pope Francis Portrait (203)
Paolo Bona	Five Cardinals (48-49)
Christian Vinces	Alfajores (89)
Anna Sofia Peláez	Pizza a Caballo (42)
Daniele da Volterra	Michelangelo (105)
Georgios Kollidas	Raphael (105)
Matteo Volpone	Vatican City (110-111)
Zvonmir Atletic	St. Martin of Tours tympanum (112)
Brother Klaus Museum	St. Nicholas of Flüe (113)
Javi Indy	The Pietà (128-129)
Sahachat Saneha	Momo Spiral Staircase (138)
Marcovarro	Sistine Chapel Detail 1 (139)
FrameAngel	Sistine Chapel Detail 2 (139)
Vladimir Wrangel	Lacoön and His Sons (148)
Asier Villafranca	Angel Playing Lute (149)
S-F	Gallery Ceiling at Vatican Museums (150-151)
Anilah	Gold Window (158-159)
EzeePics	St. Michael the Archangel (164-165)
AMB	Castel Gandolfo (170)
Angelo Giampiccolo	Frascati (171)
Catarina Belova	Streets of Rome (180-181)
Perla Berlant Wilder	Insalata di Gamberi (184)
Mi Ti	Risotto and Artichokes (187)
Filippo Monteforte	Pope Francis Prays (197)
Fotografiecor.nl	Vatican Angel (198)
Sadik Gulec	Children's Hands (203)
Nadeza Zanitaeva	Pope Benedict XVI (4)
M. Bonotto	Pope Benedict XVI portrait (44)

JOIN THE SWISS GUARD . . .

We hope you are pleased with *Pontifical Swiss Guard presents The Vatican Cookbook* and will continue to enjoy the recipes and histories, tributes and portraits that we offer for years to come.

As we close the Book with prayers of thanks for our food and all the blessings we receive, we extend an invitation and a humble request to all. We invite you to join the Swiss Guard.

Yes, join the Swiss Guard now and support the campaign to end hunger in the world. Led by Caritas Internationalis and joined by more than 100 humanitarian organizations working in 160 nations to fight hunger on every front, *One Human Family, Food for All* is the first ever comprehensive global campaign to eradicate hunger. The campaign has already made good progress in the efforts to:

    Provide urgently needed food in crisis areas and emergency situations anywhere in the world
    Develop seed bank and irrigation programs to promote sustainability and self-sufficiency
    Initiate education programs to improve food production quality and reduce food waste
    Work with governments worldwide to guarantee the right to food for all.

The Pontifical Swiss Guard is proud to stand in solidarity with Pope Francis and Caritas Internationalis and swear our support to the *One Human Family, Food for All* campaign to end hunger in the world by 2025.

ONE HUMAN FAMILY, FOOD FOR ALL

Can we really end hunger in the world?

Yes, we can. Thanks to the charitable efforts of Caritas Internationalis and many others, the number of hungry people in the world has decreased by 100 million over the past 25 years. This is a promising start, but a long way to go. More than 800 million are suffering from chronic hunger and malnutrition today.

We have the food, the resources and the systems in place to feed the world. All we need is your help to provide food for all ... today, tomorrow and forever.

In a world with so much wealth and so many resources, enough to feed everyone, it is unfathomable that there are so many hungry children.

Today, I am pleased to announce the launch of a campaign against global hunger by our very own Caritas Internationalis, and to tell you that I give my full support.

POPE FRANCIS (2013)

Please help support one human family, food for all

Catholic Relief Services (CRS) is a founding member of Caritas Internationalis. Donations to *One Human Family, Food for All* through CRS are tax deductible for U.S. citizens.

Support the *One Human Family, Food for All* campaign in the USA by donating to CRS at:

> **ONLINE:** donate.crs.org
> **MAIL:** Catholic Relief Services, PO Box 17090, Baltimore, MD 21297-0303

> **CONTACT:** Caritas Internationalis at **caritas.org** for giving in other nations.